# THE MILLIONAIRE WITHIN US

BY

CHRIS CARLEY

E.F. Press
404 E. 1st. St. Ste. 1396
Long Beach CA 90802
www.enlightenedpress.us

Ordering Information:
Quantity sales. Special discounts are available on quantity purchases by corporations, associations, and others. For details, contact the publisher at the address above. Orders by U.S. trade bookstores and wholesalers.

Please contact E.F. Press:
email info@enlightenedpress.us

Printed in the United States of America

ISBN 978-0-9666245-3-3

First Edition

DEDICATED TO:

*Dad.*

*I miss you so much.*

# Contents

# ACKNOWLEDGEMENTS

Thanks to Anthony Powell who reached out and gave me a hand when I was drowning in grief as my father was sick and dying. You encouraged me to finish this book, reminded me of my purpose to help others who are struggling in their businesses, dragged me through Australia and helped me to laugh again.

Thanks to my little sister Becky and Mom for taking care of me when life got rough, instilling in me the Power of God and always cheering me on.

And thanks to the other men in my life who taught me so much: Jim Rohn, Donald Trump and my dear Grandfathers Floyd Carley SR. and Dean Holgate who gave me my values and strong work ethics. Thank you to my fifth and sixth grade teachers at Chinook Elementary in Auburn, WA; Mr. Kurt Aust and Mr. Rollins for loving all my short stories, encouraging me to keep writing and believing in me. A big thanks to Don Dedo for introducing me to the best publisher and editor Noble DraKoln, along with his team at Enlightened Financial Press, who went through 1,927 pages of my writing to not only bring this book to fruition, but two more that will be available soon.

Last but never, ever least, thank you Bob Anderson for motivating me to write my lead book and first package system that helped so many make 6 figure incomes in their first year of utilizing your and Joe Flaherty's ideas, allowing me to make my first million so quickly and over 20 mill to date. You are truly one in a million.

# FOREWORD

When deciding to have the foreword done I reached out to various business associates to write it for me. Then it hit me. There is no better foreword than to show you what my life looked like years ago. Here is a page ripped from my diary. It shares with you a glimpse of who I was. In this way I am letting my past self write the foreword for this book. I want to encourage everyone, no matter what your circumstances are, that you can realize your dreams too.

From Chris Carley's Diary

October, 1987.

*I am dying.*

*I cannot bear to go to work. I have been here for three years and I have lost my life. Each night, when the alarm goes off at ten, startling me out of dreams of sunshine, white knights and laughter from childhood books and stories of what I thought my life would be, tears run out the corners of my raw red eyes as reality envelopes me. Cold, depressed, I drag myself from our mattress that sits on the floor and stumble into the small, cold bathroom. Pulling on cheap, ugly, gray sweats and the warmest coat I have, I rush out of the 600 sq. ft. broken-down apartment, maneuvering fast down the icy, wooden steps, body shivering teeth chattering, hitting sensitive back molars in some foreign, static tune that's uncontrollable. My rusted, dilapidated 'beater' parked on the street, is frozen, fresh snow hiding it and my knuckles* *are still raw from scraping ice yesterday morning and the evening before after my gloves were stolen. I pour cold water over the pitted car's windshield to melt the ice quickly, because I cannot be late again. For three years I have worked the Grave Yard shift--midnight to 7 a.m.--a prisoner in a factory. All night, while the rest of the city sleeps, I walk back and forth across freezing airplane hangars, moving heavy tools from machine to machine, my back hunched and aching. My feet throb and blisters form on top of each other, because my old tennis shoes, ensconced in bright yellow bulky toe protectors, pinch and rub causing me to limp. I cannot afford the $110 for steel-toed boots. At 28, my back is hunched and permanently aches from pushing a heavy, loaded cart of tools from machine to machine. The 'safety' glasses the company provides are flimsy and flying, toxic shavings of aluminum dust rub a red sore on the bridge of my nose and collect in my hair. The earplugs they give for protection are worthless against the roar of tons of steel being bent and piled by Goliath, monster machines lined up in each row. The shop is grimy, chemicals are used everywhere and I wear a mask but I can smell and taste the poisonous grit. Each hour passes painfully slow, until the lunch bell shrieks above the grinding of the steel, and I race to find a place to sleep on a hard, wooden bench in the bathroom. If I get there before some other sleep deprived zombie, I wolf down whatever food I brought from home and stretch out, exhausted on the ridged wood, trying to sleep, jerking and twisting, for the rest of my half hour lunch. Later, during the two, ten-minute breaks per shift that Union strikes have given us, I'll collapse on any chair near me and try to sleep. Finally, In the morning, when the bell blares signaling my agony is over, I stand in a line behind fifty or more workers, punch out by running my picture ID card thru the time* *clock and go straight to a 2 hour blue-printing class so that I may someday make more than my $10.50 an hour. After taxes, for those grueling, health-stealing hours, I take home only $5.35 for these life-sucking nights. I am forced to work every weekend for the next half year to year of my life--just as my sisters do, my father and his father before him. Saturday's work will pay Sunday's taxes.*

*After a class I do not understand, I drive back to my small, dark studio apartment that sits next to the highway, drop my clothes on the floor, freezing again because the furnace is off to save money, huddle deep into the covers, so tired I just lay there and weep. My clothes for the month are unwashed, thrown in the corner; I have not had time to grocery shop, pay my bills, or run errands but I am too depressed to care. My body is sick from the unbalanced sleep zones and it will take me a couple of anxious hours to fall asleep where I dream that I am successful, playing golf with celebrities, living in a mansion where the sun is always shinning and then woken by the alarm and it's cruelty. All the books that council visualizing the life you want are lies, torturous and cruel. Dreaming does not make it real. I do not know how to get out of this. I do not understand how I ended up here. I do not want to live. My mother is afraid that I might hurt myself. She quoted me: "As a man thinketh; so is he." What does that mean? She gave me an old book: 'Think and Grow Rich', but I do NOT understand. My thoughts create My reality? I brought it to work with me and studied it during every break and lunch, closing my eyes and picturing a beautiful life until I came back to my area and found that the women who work beside me had destroyed the pages, writing horrible, untrue and demeaning words and: 'We Thinketh YOU are a slut! You will never be rich and you will DIE here an old woman'. All my life I have believed in a 'White Knight' and being 'swept off my feet' so how did I end up in a dungeon with ugly step sisters around me?*

*This is my life? What happened to my goals and dreams of adventure and beautiful Castles? I might as well be in jail. I am in jail. No, I am in hell. I reset my alarm clock and fall into a fitful light sleep so I can get up and do it again tomorrow, and the next day, and the next day after that. There is no end. I cannot live like this.*

# *Ambition*

***Iconoclastic***

*[somebody who challenges or overturns traditional beliefs, customs, and values attacking generally accepted beliefs, customs, and opinions. attacking the beliefs, customs, and opinions that most people in a society accept. Breaks from the norm. Innovator. Rule breaker. Ground shaker. ]*

# CHAPTER 1

# ADVENTURES OF A DIRECT SALES MARKETER

Success, money, happiness does not come just to special, talented or lucky people. Within all of us lie the answers and directions we need to create unlimited abundance and you can choose a path that is joyful and easy to realize your dreams. I hope through reading my story and the lessons I have learned about marketing yourself and your business you will experience the same success results I did. If you follow the "basic marketing rules" outlined throughout this book and combine it with the "Laws of Attraction," nothing can stop you.

## MY SUCCESS WAS HARD EARNED

A lot of people look at the success that I have had in the network marketing industry and think it came from nowhere. For years I struggled unsuccessfully in business endeavors that didn't work, because I wasn't tapped into the "Universal Intelligence" that directs us all, if we let it. All my life, everyone I knew was grouped on the edge of financial ruin, working hard, long hours for big corporations that would lay our bread winners off, and/or cause hardship through months of striking without pay. Fear and uncertainty were with us at all times.

When I was younger, my parents moved us out on a farm that wasn't anything fancy, but it was a far cry from the city life I knew. It was also the first place I began to exercise my entrepreneurial creativity.

## DIRECT SALES AND THE MAN

At least two hours, twice a week, plus anytime I was in trouble and sentenced to my room for doing something I wasn't suppose to, I dreamed of ways to make money so my father wouldn't have to work so hard and could be with us more often. One of those weeks I took all of my savings, from mowing the lawn to picking berries during the summer, to invest in one little expensive vial of pure cinnamon oil. I took the oil and soaked toothpicks it, making cinnamon toothpicks, which was all the craze. I ended up selling them at school for a penny a piece.

I did so well that 20 to 30 kids were sucking on them at recess. thirty cents, may not be a big deal now, but it was the world to me and I could feel I was onto something. Well, that same day some of the teachers took notice. They began to worry that someone might fall and choke on one. I'm not sure who it was, but one my classmates ratted me out to my teacher and I promptly found myself sitting in the principal's office.

Now you have to understand, in my family, being sent to the principal's office meant double punishment. My legs were shaking and my face was bright red as I stumbled into his office. I knew that the next thing that was going to happen was a call to my parents, and I hated disappointing them.

The principal sat me down, paused, and looked at me for a moment. Then he spoke, "Christine, I am proud of your business skills, but the teachers are worried the kids will get hurt with the toothpicks, would you please stop selling them at school." Relief spread across my chest. I nodded yes and quickly got out of there. I still needed to figure out how to make money though.

## WALNUTS TAUGHT ME EVERYTHING

The next project was buying a calf for 4H. Attending the meetings at my friends' homes was embarrassing. They all had top bred, prize winning animals, and I had nothing. My parents told me I could join, but they weren't buying me any kind of animal until I proved that I was committed to the 4H cause.

So every month I would attend the 4-H meetings mortified. I would stand there, pretending I had a calf. As the others were shown how to clean the hooves and ears of their calves, I would listen intently and go through the motions on my pretend calf. While they were being taught the general care of their steers and heifers, I could see some of the kids making fun of me, a few even turned the garden hose towards me to irritate me. Nevertheless, I was determined.

The chance to redeem myself came in the form of nuts, bags and bags of walnuts. 4H was having a fund-raising drive to benefit the local fair. All of the members had to sell bags of walnuts, even the ones with calves. I was born competitive and although I wasn't excited aboutselling walnuts, I *pictured* myself selling the most.

I knew that I wanted to win the contest, so I began by asking my mom if she needed any walnuts for her brownies or cookies. Half expecting her to say no, I told her what the walnuts' price per pound was. I had never seen my mom so enthusiastic. On the spot she bought all of my bags of walnuts. Then she asked me if I could get more. I grinned. In that moment I felt like I had a chance at winning.

The next day she drove me back to the farm of our 4H leader. The woman looked amazed that I had sold everything and already needed more. Handing her the cash, I asked for double the amount this time. Her words shook my confidence. "Are you sure? You're awful little to be handling so many walnuts." My face burned bright red and I just stood there, staring at her, saying nothing.

"How 'bout we give you just a couple pounds again and see how you do." Standing there, looking at the ground I just nodded, took what she gave me and headed back to the car. Mom saw the look on my face, the small bag of walnuts and said, "You go back in there and tell her you need more."

"I did. She wouldn't give them to me. She said I was too little."

"Come on." Mom, in her bathrobe and slippers, marched across the wet grass towards the barn. I ran behind. I was so happy to have my mom sticking up for me.

The 4H leader's farm was nothing like ours. Everything shone new in the morning sun. Her fence was perfect and bright white, which matched the barn's trim. $10,000 prized bulls and award winning Black Angus cattle munched on expensive hay. The bulls and cattle lazily turned their heads to look at us with curious eyes. My mom approached the 4H leader, who was now brushing down a pure-blood, nervous race horse and said, "Excuse me. I just took the time to drive my daughter over here so she could get more walnuts to sell."

Shocked by my mom's irritation, the 4H leader stopped brushing the horse and turned to my mom. Before she could say anything, mom said, "You don't know my daughter, but I do, and she would like 30 more pounds of walnuts, please."

"Sure." The lady said with a smile. "There's no bringing them back, you know."

Finally, my anger at her snide remarked allowed me to stick up for myself. "Have any of the other kids sold all their walnuts you gave us last night?" I asked.

"Well, no, but I'm sure..." Seeing the determination in me she handed over the 30 pounds of walnuts to me. I carried them all to the car, staggering under the weight.

"She can't even lift them!" The woman pointed out to my mom.

Ignoring the woman, mom marched back to the car, head down, dodging manure land mines.

"You have to understand what you have here. Good walnuts are hard to come by and every mother or wife is baking cookies, pies, brownies—all kinds of things this summer."

Eager, I opened up the glove compartment, got some paper out and found an old pen and started to add to mom's list of all the things walnuts could be used for. Banana bread, fudge, over salads, on ice-cream, cereal, carrot cake. Then I made a list of everyone I knew who might want to buy walnuts from me. Living out of town on a farm with only a few neighbors was not going to slow me down.

I began writing. Grandma cooked a lot, grandma's friends cooked stuff with walnuts, all the ladies at church, a new neighbor with four kids had just moved in...

"You know, I could drop you off in different neighborhoods across town and you could go door-to-door..."

"Ok, after I get everyone out here where there are no grocery stores," I said. Mom smile.

***

As soon as we got home, I tied a bag of walnuts to my bike's handlebars and on the back fender. I also picked up one in my arms and planned to ride one-handed, but decided against that after I crashed. Going to the only three neighbors in our area, I had a warm reception. After my carefully planned pitch of all the things they could use walnuts for, each woman smiled and laughed. In fact, they all wanted a bag.

Then I upsold them, (I didn't know what that was back then), making sure to let them know that I was the youngest and smallest kid in 4H who had already sold the most walnuts, capping it off by saying, "And I'm going to win first prize." That made the women buy another bag, and they didn't even care when I told them... I didn't even know what the first prize was. Then I asked if they knew anyone at their church, work or any family members that might want walnuts. Instinctively I had asked for referrals. They were glad to give me phone numbers of people they knew would want them.

Both of my grandmas bought 5 bags each. My maternal grandmother gave me the telephone numbers of her friends. As a kid I hated calling or even talking to someone I didn't know on the telephone—but I forced myself to dial the numbers. Even though I stuttered when I made my pitch, I sold all four of grandma's friends.

The next day, when we showed back up at the 4H leader's house, she didn't say a word as I handed her the money and asked for double the amount of bags again. The contest only lasted until the end of summer and mom had dad take some bags to work and I wrote up a little paper on all the things walnuts could be used for, for him to show his coworkers. Mom drove me to Seattle to deliver grandma Carley's walnuts. Nan had a list of her friends that lived nearby and grandpa heard that dad had sold 5 bags so he bought 7 bags from me to sell at work the next day. Gramps was really helpful too.

One day, when I went with mom to get groceries, I saw some of the older kids who had made fun of me for not having a calf trying to sell their walnuts outside the store. They looked miserable. They obviously had been there for a while, because their clothes were sweaty and their faces sunburned and it looked like none of them had sold a thing.

## LESSONS LEARNED AND SHARED

- √ Don't let anyone steal your dreams. Get your family and loved ones to believe in you by showing determination. That 4H lady didn't believe in me, but instead of letting that stop me, I let it make me more passionate about succeeding.
- √ Know your product. Sell something that is consumable and that you are excited about.
- √ You will have difficulties, but when you understand that every successful sales person and company had those same obstacles and overcame them, then you can too.
- √ To get more, you need to become more. The only way to do that is to study and learn your craft. Before you get on the phone to anyone, spend at least 15 minutes on HOW TO tap into the Universal Intelligence. Get the book "The Magic of Believing" by Claude Bristol and "TNT it Rocks the Earth." Those words will change your entire day and allow you to attract easily and effortlessly.

# CHAPTER

# 2

# PICTURE THIS

Imagine a woman, dead broke with over $30,000 in debt. A woman in a horrible, unsatisfying marriage, a woman who's health was so bad that she couldn't get out of bed some days. That was me. I was a long way from the little girl who excitedly sold walnuts for 4H that one summer. I don't say this for you to have sympathy or to feel bad for me. In fact I want you to celebrate with me and see that if I could make that first step toward changing my circumstances, so can you.

At that time in my life all of my friends and family were steering clear of me. I had lost my hostile work environment case against Boeing and owed my attorneys over $30,000. Earlier business opportunities I had introduced to my family and friends had failed miserably. I felt it was because of my lack of experience, education, and my eroding self esteem. I felt toxic and for the first time in my life, not only was I out of shape, I was also fat. I wanted to and needed to make a change, but I didn't know how to start. I began praying and asking for guidance and right away I started remembering from my grade school years a teacher that had told us about how words affect us. I realized I had been telling myself the wrong story.

## THE MIND BODY CONNECTION

In the movie, *Out of Africa*, Robert Redford tells Meryl Streep that when men from African tribes were put into captivity they died, because they couldn't understand that one day they would be released. I think people who commit suicide must feel that way too. Books on depression reveal that suicidal thoughts are often contemplated by persons experiencing debilitating waves of despair when they do not think the future will be any different. Lying on the couch for months, hour after hour after hour reliving my failures, losses and unfair circumstances, vegetating in front of the television, depression engulfed me heavily, so painfully that I could not bear it anymore. Going to a doctor and spending an hour talking about my problems and re-experiencing the awful feelings of hopelessness, worrying out loud that each day for the rest of my life would be the same, the misery never going away, that I would always be like this, I'd never laugh again, or feel good or want to do anything, or be passionate about something ever in my life, left me feeling even worse. I'd come out of the psychiatrist's office shaking, crying sometimes throwing up.

The more the doctor had me talk about bad experiences, the more I noticed the world's hardships. What is the reason any of us are even here? What is my purpose? What am I supposed to be doing here? If there really is a reason for everything that happens, what is it?!

Sick of myself, tired of the couch, I rolled to my knees and prayed for understanding, waited, and when nothing happened, no ideas or booming voice from the heavens answered, I flopped on the floor defeated, tears rolling out of the corners of red, swollen eyes. *How can I have any tears left? What happened to that girl who hit home runs so easily?*

Since the verdict, I had done nothing but cram food down my throat and I was easily 40 pounds overweight, disgustedly pushing the scales at 170 pounds. Everything I read about depression said exercise and changing negative thoughts to positive would snap the afflicted back to 'normal'.

Dragging myself off the tear-stained rug, I searched through the month-long scattered clothes trying to find something warm to wear so I wouldn't freeze, my bed calling me to come back. I tried desperately to think of anything good in my life. Nothing.Then a glimmer of some forgotten fragment buried deep in my brain started to surface and I remembered segments of a book I had been reading during my lunches at Boeing.

## CHANGE YOUR THOUGHTS

As I focused the minute thought grew, bringing to mind, '....you are what you think about.' This memory brought forth old, tiny feelings of confidence and energy I possessed back before I lost my job at Boeing and I saw my old self bent over a book, scribbling furiously on my notepad, underlining passages, unaware of anything or anyone, smiling whenever I read something that really struck home.

The book had been very old, written in 1930 but I couldn't remember the name. If I could relive every detail of bad times, couldn't I do the same with the times I'd felt good? Forgetting present time, I felt the coldness of the shop, the isolating breaks that had allowed me to study human psych for years, zoomed in on the title, but could only 'see' the author's name: Claude Bristol. Instantly I recalled the title, "The Magic of Believing". Eerily the book's words flooded not only my intellect, but my body. The entire premise of the old book taught that anyone could think their way into better circumstances thus changing their lives. Zig Ziglar had written an introduction telling the reader: "...this little book....changed my life from poverty, despair and defeat into happiness and richness beyond imagination."

Running to my boxes of books, I found it on the top and opening it, again the words hit me in the face. *"For those of you who seek to learn and make progress, I gently lay this message in your laps. I do so without the slightest fear but that it will turn your world entirely upside down—bringing you health, wealth, success and happiness, provided you understand and accept it."*

Reading the words, I remembered why I had been selected out of thousands of smarter people trying out for Wheel of Fortune! For months, I had concentrated on seeing myself winning on the show. I wasn't worried about not making the cut, because I had pictured myself *spinning the wheel* and winning!

*"This power can be proved by the teachings of the Bible, certain well-established laws of physics and, last but not least, just plain common sense."*

How could I have forgotten this?

*Because for the last two years ALL your thoughts have been focused on the horrible atrocities that surrounded you daily at work and then again in court,* I answered myself, then, *'keep reading'* came into my head and I continued. *"Nothing in this world is so powerful as an idea whose time has come."*—Victor Hugo.

Wow! That had been the answer to the puzzle on Wheel Of Fortune that I had won so much money from! Goosebumps exploded on my arm, the hair standing straight up.

*"The time has come for the greatest idea in the world to take possession of your consciousness. It is a simple idea, but when you open up your mind and let it in, you'll never be the same again."* This is why I had been fired from a job that almost killed me. There was a better place for me than that factory job! I hadn't forgotten any of it; it had always been there in my brain cells, but had temporarily disappeared *from lack of use.*

## SERVING MY TIME AT BOEING

My brain, now fired and working fast, flashed me back to the memory of reading these same books during lunch. A new co-worker about my mother's age that I was training, we will call her "Janet", had just left the lunch group of hateful girls and had walked back to our area. Lighting a cigarette, blowing smoke at me, knowing I was deathly allergic to it, she looked at the book and laughed, shaking her perfectly coiffed, bleached blonde, mother-beehive styled head.

"What?" I challenged.

Chuckle, chuckle, chuckle, roll of the eyes, shake of the head, "Chris, you're NOT special."

Startled, her mean words hit me. "Did you really just say that?" I choked.

Flicking her cigarette ashes at me, she pointed to my

book. "Every day I see you reading those books thinking that they'll help you get out of here, but you won't. You're just like all of us and 30 years from now you'll still be here."

I opened another book I'd studied, Charles Haanel's Master Key System. "Janet, this book was written in the 40's and the same principal is used in every book on success; including the bible. It's a scientific fact that our bodies are made up of atoms and our thoughts affect—"

Pushing the book away, she got into my face, her yellow teeth and bad smoke breath forcing me to recoil. "LISTEN to me. YOU ARE NOBODY SPECIAL. It's a joke that you think you'll be the "one" that makes it out of here."

"Come on Janet! There are millions of people who are thriving, who have second and third homes. All we have to do is find out what they know and do it."

Still shaking her head, she ignored me, pushing her cart down to where the gaggle of negative women still congregated, replaying our conversation to them, peals of shrill laughter heard all over the shop.Going in the opposite direction to work in a connecting building, I felt myself slowing down and my shoulders sinking. There wasn't anyone in my life I could even talk to about these books. I felt churning in my stomach and a knot tightening—good old FEAR—would I really be here the next 30 years? My father had and his father before him.

As anxiousness and trepidation flooded through me, my body began to change chemically. My heart rate dropped, my facial muscles slackened, and my movement became clumsy. The clock ticked more slowly, but the last paragraph I was reading before Janet rudely slapped it out of my hands hit me, so I ducked into the bathroom to read it again.

"FACT: *We all have over a trillion cells in our bodies with each cell having its own consciousness. When the brain is given a thought from our mind, the cerebro-spinal system of nerves puts conscious communication with every part of our body based on whatever thought we are thinking. The system of nerves responds to every sensation: taste, sound, pain, light, heat, cold. Whatever thoughts we send to the cerebro-spinal nervous system determines what our body feels and reacts*."

This made sense to me. If I think of biting into a peeled lemon, really chomping on it, instantly my mouth starts to water! My face scrunches up, I have to swallow. This proved that thoughts didn't have to be *real* for our bodies to react. My body automatically responded to the thought! *If I think sad and depressing thoughts, I feel bad, and my body responds. If I think about good stuff—*

## TRYING TO SQUASH THAT NEGATIVE INNER VOICE

I remember so clearly at the time the two voices that were waging an internal war within me. I started to argue with myself.

*But there isn't any good in my life now. I've got a job I hate. My life is awful.*

*You've got two arms and two legs. You are in shape.* Some thing, some energy answered.

*I have a loveless, lousy marriage and working midnight to seven is making me sick.*

*You've done it before—been successful in starting your own trucking business.*

*But... I lost everything!*

*You had no control over the oilfield crashing. You've learned from it! You are still young!*

*Oh God what am I going to do to get out of here?*

Flipping through the pages I got the answer and read:

You do not need to know the HOW, you need only visualize, dwell upon the outcome wanted.

*But it hurts to think about what I don't have.*

*Just do it.*

I could clomp through work focusing on what Janet had said, get upset or I could follow through with what every bestseller taught and replace my negative fears.

*Okay, where do I start...? I know what I don't want... What do I want? I want to have a job where I change people's lives and make a lot of money. I want to be a millionaire, living in Malibu, CA,* ***on*** *the beach, in the sun.* I left the bathroom feeling better.

I began to picture in detail a big, white, wide-open beachfront home, with the ocean as my front yard. It didn't work. Doubts and fear and the sensation of grief swallowed me whole and I ducked into an empty office sobbing, shoulders shaking, hopelessness weighing me down until I was sitting on the cold, filthy cement floor. 'It' wasn't working. There is no way my dreams were going to happen here and my body wasn't fooled by the thought, in fact it seemed mad. I understood I wasn't to worry about the 'how' part of it, to keep picturing what I want and then listen if I get an idea or inspiration to do something, but from the dungeon I'm trapped in here to a place in Malibu? Maybe I should focus on something smaller, like a better job or seeing myself living in a sunshine filled state.

As I did my menial job I started to picture myself

happy and walking along a beach. Three hours later when the alarm for our last ten minute break sounded, I grabbed my book and opened it. I sat frozen. On almost every page, something awful and obscene had been written in thick black permanent ink. Those awful girls watched from a distance laughing. This time I felt sorry for them. They would be here for the next 30 years. I would not.

Ignoring them, I opened the book and read:

*"....this idea will shake you to the foundations of your being. It will destroy old false concepts and replace them with new ones. It will eventually remove fear and worry from your life. It will release you from chronic nervous tensions, chase the butterflies out of your stomach, restore your self-confidence, give you a more positive attitude and enable you to face things you've been running away from, for years!"*

## MOVING FORWARD

Like working out, at first you don't feel the full effects immediately. Sometimes I was still disillusioned with society, so sad about the future for all those women left in a toxic work environment, earning less pay for the same job and losing earned promotions to incompetent males. When the negative thoughts wouldn't leave me, I hung my head and prayed for guidance. It shocked me, nearly knocking me over when help came right away, the Voice, again, inside my head. (God? A Higher Power? The Universe? My own subconscious?) instructing me:

"Go for a walk."

After losing my job I had been so depressed it was hard to get out of bed. How the hell was I to go for a walk when I couldn't even get dressed, take a shower or get off the couch? I had been living in my sweats and my next thought or Voice, prompted me to just slip on my clumsy Ugg boots, walk to the door, open the door, walk down the short flight of stairs, through the small parking lot, and to the mailbox.

Because I wanted to shut up the now nagging voice and I also wanted to put off looking for a job, I grabbed my house keys, shoved on the boots, and for some reason picked up my wallet and clomped down the stairs. My body screamed, "Turn back.Wheel of Fortune is on; let's just watch it for a little bit, take a small nap first and then we'll go for a walk"

Usually this worked but surprisingly I quickly countered with "All we have to do is walk to the mailbox and then you can do anything you want and eat anything you want." The promise of a 'fix' of something fattening and sugary must have flooded my brain with endorphins because I flew down the stairs and made it to the mailboxes in record time.

For once, it was a beautiful day in Seattle. The sun had come out momentarily and although it was still drizzling, little warm rays hit my back, promising a hint of Spring. I stretched, turning my pale face upwards, breathing deeply, the heavy, achy cloud of despair withdrawing a teeny, tiny bit.

Looking around, bright green and small yellow and pink buds everywhere copied me, reaching hard for that teasing warmth of a small sunshine patch, tired from the last *eight months* of gloomy, gray rain. Taking a bigger breath through my nose, my lungs filled and the smell of pine, forest muskiness and, coming from somewhere- - my favorite scent -- sweet, heavy, lilac.

Getting out from under the shadows of the

apartments, forcing heavy legs and sluggish limbs, finally feeling a bit of life awakening inside myself, I didn't hesitate when I reached the sidewalk and fixated on my goal, just a little farther down, the main road to our apartment club house.

## HOW IT ALL STARTED

The books said that all I had to do was picture the end result I wanted and then the right people and opportunities would come my way. It was very difficult at first to keep images of being successful when reality of not having a job, being in debt were staring at me daily, but as I practiced seeing my end results I got better and better at it. When I was first called to answer an ad, that was direct mailed to me on a health/weight loss product, the guy that placed the ad said to me, 'How fat are you?' I was so stunned; I just hung up on him. THAT GUY TODAY HAS LOST MILLIONS BECAUSE HE DIDN'T KNOW HOW TO ANSWER THE PHONE.

A short time later I responded to another ad that was under "Help Wanted" in the local paper that said: We pay you to lose weight. $1,700 to $4,000 per month full time and part time positions.

"I'm calling about your ad." I asked, hopeful that he would be professional. "Can I have your name please?"

This threw me off because I didn't want to give out my personal information until I knew what this was all about. I stuttered, "I'm...I'm... ca...calling about *your* ad. I. Just. Want. Some. Information."

"And *I*, would just like your name."

Speechless, embarrassed to tell him who the fat girl was that was calling until I knew who he was and what the job entailed, I just sat there and he finally said, "Well, I'll tell you my name then. My name is Dave, what is your name?"

"Uh...my name is Sarah." I stumbled, saying the first fake name that came to me not understanding why I was lying.

"Sarah, do you have a last name?"

Why didn't he just tell me about the job?

"Look, I'm calling for some information about the job you have advertised. I just want some information about your company."

He started laughing at me and meanly asked, "How heavy are you?"

Didn't he understand how difficult it was for someone who knows they need to lose weight to jump right in and start telling a stranger how they let themselves go? Didn't he realize the amount of courage that same person needed to have to admit that they have hit such a low in their life, that they have to be calling someone like him?

Why didn't they have someone answering the phones that had been overweight and wasn't so condescending? Slamming the phone down wasn't good enough and I picked it up and slammed it twice more.

That guy would also lose millions of dollars again because he didn't understand "Basic Marketing".

Opening another paper I saw the same ad with a different number. This time I heard, "Hi, this is John. Can I help you?"

"Yes. Have you hired the 29 people yet for losing weight?"

"No, we haven't, are you interested?"

"How many positions do you have left?"

Faltering, he paused and then answered, "Uh...we have...21 positions left."

"Can you tell me a little bit about your company?"

"Sure. What is your name?"

Frustrated, angry, each word clipped I said again, "Can you just *please* tell me about your company!"

"We are a 15 year old nutritional company and do business in 45 different countries."

Finally! "Great. How much are you paying?"

"Well...," he stammered, "How many pounds do you want to lose?"

Why couldn't he just tell me how much the position paid? Embarrassed, I answered, stiffly, "Fifty."

"Okay." He seemed relieved. "What is your name and address?"

What the hell is going on? What kind of company asked questions like this? Shouldn't there be an interview? Was there even a position available? Wasn't this illegal?

"Can. You." I demanded, saying each word slowly, "Please. Tell me HOW I get paid to lose weight?"

Silence and then, "Well, we set up an appointment with you and you come down and meet us--" I cut him off, furious now.

"Why won't you tell me how much this job pays?"

Finally, embarrassed he said, "Our packages start at $200 and..."

"I'm calling *about a job* to lose weight and you want me to pay *you* $200?!" I shouted. "Don't you think if I had $200, I wouldn't be calling you asking for a job?"

Unbelievable! What a scam. How could they do this to people who needed to lose weight and wanted to work?

"Once you start taking the product and you lose weight, you'll be able to sell it to your friends and family." He hurriedly read from a script.

"Greaaa----at," I said, sarcastically drawing out the word. "And your product, does it really work?"

"Absolutely!" He exclaimed. Excited now, he rolled into his canned pitch. "We've had thousands lose weight and are now making $10,000 a month!"

Come on! What kind of scam was this? "Then how about YOU give me your product and when I lose the weight, I'll start selling it and pay you back the $200?" I asked.

"We don't do it that way."

"If you really believe in this product and if you are really making 10 grand a month, then why wouldn't you?"

Silence.

Angrily, I answered for him, "Of course you don't do business this way, You. Are. A. Scam. Someone who goes after people who are at their worse and have nowhere else to go."

Smashing the phone back into the cradle again, I starting crying, ashamed of myself—ashamed that I had let myself go, ashamed that I was so stupid thinking that there might be a company out there that would really help someone like me.

***

Weeks went by and I called another weight loss ad that was mailed to my home. It came in an envelope with a bunch of other flyers for laundry service, local restaurants, cable service etc. It said that the product was money-back guaranteed, $30.00 and ‘free samples’. I thought to myself, now or never.

I called, but I kept getting an answering machine that didn’t give me any information. I hung up three times over the next two days. Finally I left my name and number. After a week went by, I saw the same ad in the local paper and decided to call it.

“Lose weight, feel great. This is Linda.”

“Hi, I’m calling about your ad and your free samples.”

“Great! I lost 8 lbs. in two weeks. It’s 100% natural, $30.00 and has a money-back guarantee. I can take your credit card information and you can get it in the mail in just a few days or you can come by.” I didn’t have a credit card so she told me if I would put a check in the mail today, she would send out the product. She had made it easy. I also learned what an effective sale looked like that day.

## LESSONS LEARNED AND SHARED

√ Learn how to answer your phone correctly. Understand that the second you start talking, you are training that person. If you don’t make it simple, fun and easy, that person will think they can never do what you are doing. Tell your success story first. Talk about what your product has done for you and your loved ones.

√ Identify with the person. Know success stories of truckers, waitresses, single mothers, professionals.

√ Sell and advertise a low cost product to get your foot in the door then listen to the person and plant a seed of upgrades, referrals and working with you WHEN they get a product result.

# CHAPTER

# 3

# MY JOURNEY

I began to use my supply of herbs and I could feel the little tablets kicking in right away, that hour, feeding my brain, nourishing my starved body. As I started to feel better, I began to remember all the things that I had pushed aside and had actually done really well at.

My inner voice was saying to me, *"You were picked out of 15,000 people and made it on Wheel of Fortune! YOU WON $33,300, beating the best competitors nationwide, at the lowest time in life. You started an "all girl" trucking company and you bought and owned 2 houses before you were 22! You got yourself and your husband hired at Boeing when they weren't even hiring. You attended classes every night after working 8-hour shifts and weekends at Boeing. You did all that!"*

Instead of sleeping in, depressed, I was jumping out of bed early, doing the Rocky dance and that morning I jammed on my sweats and for the first time in a long time, I walked the 2 miles to the gym.

## DOWN THE RABBIT HOLE

Because I couldn't afford to buy the books that would teach me HOW, I lived at the library and began reading up on the 21 different herbs that were in the pills I was taking. I researched each one and became excited when I found out one of the herbs, Valerian, helped depression. Some of the other herbs were diuretics, and two or three were stimulants. There seemed to be a lot of controversy on the main ingredient, ma huang, but I didn't care.

I felt great and after losing 4 lbs my first week, I had lost 5 more the next week and coming up on my third week, I ran out. Squirreling away the $36 I needed from not buying junk food and beer at the grocery store, I called Linda up and agreed to drive over to her house to pick them up so I could get them that day.

Normally, I would have hated to leave my apartment to go anywhere, but I was feeling so good it didn't bother me and I was turning into her neighborhood a half hour later. Looking up from my driving notes I pulled over thinking I had taken a wrong turn somewhere. The homes were beautiful, in the $300,000 range, big money for me at the time, and I drove back to the nearest strip mall to find a telephone booth and called her.

## AGORAPHOBIA SAVED MY LIFE

She explained that I had been in the right place, to just keep going until the end and her house would be close to the woods, on the left. Understanding now that she lived just beyond the gated homes, I got back into my rat-trap Honda and tried not to be embarrassed as I drove by these wonderful homes, hoping that no one would notice the dents in each side and the smoke coming out of the broken tail pipe.

Reaching the end of the instructions, I looked up and just stared. Her house was one of the biggest and prettiest houses on the block. I held my breath as I rang the doorbell, thinking I was still at the wrong house.

As the door opened and I saw Linda for the first time, I backed away ready to apologize to the heavy, barely dressed woman who answered. Her hair was frizzy and unkempt and her house slippers were ratty. It was 1 o'clock in the afternoon and it looked like she had just woken up.

"You must be Chris. Come in," she said, opening the door just enough to let me through. I followed her through the house, wondering why it was so dark and without thinking I said, "Is your power out?"

When she said, "I'm bulimic and an agoraphobic too." I almost bolted remembering that I hadn't told anyone where I was going, but calmed down when we entered the gorgeous kitchen.

## NEVER JUDGE A BOOK BY ITS COVER

We sat down and I rudely blurted, "I thought you told me that these products were incredible and that you had lost weight." If she had lied to me about how great this whole thing was and how much money she made and if it didn't really work, it would break me. If she took away the little bit of hope I did have that this product would help me...

"I lost over 70 pounds and my allergies cleared up, my bulimia is cleared up and I'm losing more each week."

"Didn't you tell me you had been in this company for five years?" I asked warily.

"Yes, but this new Thermogenics product just came out two months ago and people are losing weight like crazy."

I didn't want to leave without my pills so I handed her my $36.00 and she gave me back $4 since she didn't have to ship it to me.

"You know we have a lot more products, weight-loss tea, protein shakes..."

"Just the pills, please." I said firmly.

"I'll put in a few samples of the NRG tea and the shake mix." I watched her put a bunch of literature and the samples in a bag. As she did this she handed me what looked like a check.

I read, "$5,000," and asked, "What's this?"

"It's what I made last month." She answered slyly.

"Whaa, whaat, from selling these pills?" I felt dizzy.

Handing me an even bigger read out she said, "I use to make over $10,000 a month, before the United States Senate made us re-label our packaging."

I stared at the $10,000 checks from the last years, looked at Linda and then around the house. I noticed a picture of her in front of a plane.

She caught where my eyes had landed.

"I learned how to fly and bought a plane.", she said casually.

Sitting there, I started to shake and got, really excited. If this lady could earn that kind of money, with all her problems—she couldn't even leave her house for goodness sake—I would get rich.

## LESSONS LEARNED AND SHARED

√ Utilize FREE SAMPLES! In all your advertising and business cards. Give samples that the person can feel instantly.

√ SHOW your success. If you don't have any yet, show your colleagues' checks. I used dozens of $30 checks to show my customers who had experienced success to entice them into registering with the company under me.

CHAPTER

# 4

# BECOMING THE “$79”, MILLIONAIRE

After using the products, for the first time in my entire life, I had no trouble getting out of bed. The pounding of my heart startled me awake; my eyes flew open and I jumped out of bed, heading for the bathroom.

I met my eyes in the mirror and felt a rush in my solar plexus.

“*OMG*, this stuff works!” I yelled out loud.

A huge grin filled the mirror, but before I could admire it, my old self filled my thoughts. “You just *think* it is working because you want it to so much.”

Doubts flooded my thoughts, taking over the weaker, newer good thoughts, and reminded me of the thousands of studies I had read about placebos given in the war when the medics had run out of morphine.

Wounded and dying soldiers swallowing fake pills, with nothing but sugar in them and instantly feeling high, unable to feel the doctors slicing, stitching their bodies... The mind is so powerful; who cared. As long as it worked?

Taking the pills two times a day at 10:00 and 3:00 didn't work for me. They gave me so much energy that I couldn't sleep at night and so I set my alarm for 5 a.m., put four green and two beige out with a glass of water, and barely hearing the alarm, I downed the pills in my sleep.

At 7 a.m. my eyes flew open and I immediately threw off the covers and got up! Feeling great I found myself putting my stuff away that I had left on the floor, thrown in a closet, stuffed under the couch and by the time my husband came in the door 45 minutes later, instead of looking like a bomb had gone off, the apartment was inviting, welcoming and breakfast—scrambled eggs with turkey meat—was ready.

"Are you okay? I mean...the place...it looks like you're feeling better?"

Laughing nervously I replied, "I think so..." I didn't want to tell him about the pills yet, because I was afraid he would get mad about the money—or worse—make fun of the whole thing.

He was still working midnight to seven and as he got ready for bed, I got into the shower and he called through the door, "You're not going to come lay down with me?" Since I had been fired, he found me sound asleep every morning when he got off work and I'd usually be there until ten or 11:00 when I would get up and go lay down on the couch and watch TV.

"I'm going to go see Mom today and go for a walk." I could tell he was excited, hoping that the new me would last but afraid to say anything in case it knocked me back to where I had been for the last year.

## HOW I BECAME THE "$79" MILLIONAIRE

Linda explained to me if I registered with the company I could buy my pills at wholesale. I called my father and asked to borrow his credit card for a purchase of $79.00. Dad didn't mind loaning any of us money, but he made us sign a contract so there would never be any misunderstandings and to teach us to always do that in life.

"Dad, I'm taking this vitamin product that is really making me feel better—I've already lost 12 pounds—I need the money to register with the company so I can buy it wholesale and you don't have to worry, I am not going to get involved selling this stuff, I just want to get it for wholesale."

We agreed that I would pay it back monthly.

## MY FIRST 12 LEADS

This was my third month taking the pills. I headed back up to Linda's. After we finished the paperwork, she handed me a list of 12 names.

"This is a list of leads that came from the flier you saw, that I couldn't get to. They're kind of old, but you can have them."

I gave her a blank look, not understanding.

I knew how she felt; I was worried that it might happen to me again.

I knew how she felt and I was worried that it might happen to me again. Then she continued.

"I was molested as a child," she continued. "These products saved my life. I'm so much better than I was."

Back home, I checked to make sure my husband was still sleeping and took the phone to the other end of the apartment. Looking at the names on the list, I realized I didn't know what to say. I called Linda and she asked me, "Did you go through your registration kit? Everything you need to know is in there."

"Not what to say!" I'd gone through the whole thing and it was a bunch of junk, with some shake powder and two other bottles of vitamins I didn't' need.

"Just say what I said when we first talked."

This infuriated me. "That was a while ago, don't you have a script or something?"

"A script would make you sound automatic. Just talk to them."

She hung up and I sat there shaking my head. How had I fallen into this again? I didn't want to do this business and here I was doing it! I wadded the sheet up, ready to throw it away, when I remembered that I had to pay my dad back. I hesitated then remembered that I had lost 18 pounds in my first three weeks—that was all that mattered! I smoothed out the paper and called the first number. An older woman answered.

"Hi, I'm returning a call from Edna from the home mailer: Lose 30 pounds, 30 days, $30.00, my name is Chris."

Silence.

"I know it's been a while since you called—"

Irritably she broke in and said, "Two months."

"Wow, really? I'm just getting your name and number

because the woman that ran the ad is so overwhelmed she couldn't get back to everyone." Not taking a breath I continued, "I called off this very same ad and I was really skeptical. I had tried everything to lose weight and lost my money on things that didn't work, but this stuff is so incredible that I felt it the first hour—and I lost 4 pounds my first week, 6 pounds the 2nd week, then two the next week, then 7 pounds the 4th week."

"I had been depressed, I felt awful—couldn't' get off the couch—and now I have energy, I feel great and I look great!"

Taking a breath, I was ready to continue when she interrupted me. "Look, you talk so fast that I don't even know what you just said, but whatever you're on, I'll take it!"

Looking at my reflection in the apartment's big picture window—eyes wide, mouth open—I jumped up and down and did a little dance. I explained to her that I didn't have a merchant account to take her credit card and she promised to put a check in the mail that day.

## MY BIG BREAK THROUGH

Shaking, I sat back down and called all the people on the list. Out of 12 names I reached 10 people and sold nine! The one I didn't sell was upfront with me that she didn't have the $30.00. I told her about my life and how low I had been for the last year and said, "If you know three or four people that want to lose weight, you have them call me and if they buy, I'll mail yours to you for free."

The next day four of her friends called, all buying and I had to call Linda back to get product to mail out to everyone.

"You sold them all?" She asked, amazed.

"All but the two who weren't at home, but the four referrals I got made up for that." Excited, my words were coming out fast and I felt a thrill at having a product that really worked.

Linda was worried that some of the people wouldn't follow through and send their checks so she gave me her merchant account number and explained to me how to use it.

"I'll reimburse you each month, after you send me the sales information." She then gave me 15 more leads and asked if I wanted to go put up posters with her. I didn't know what she was talking about, but I said yes and she told me she'd pick me up at midnight.

We drove just a couple of miles and Linda turned on her blinker, pulling into a Kinko's Copy shop. She had an 8 x 11 master copy of a sign on regular typing paper. Lose 30lbs, $30, 30-day guarantee. I added FREE SAMPLES! To the top of it and I was in business.

## LESSONS LEARNED AND SHARED

- √ We all have excuses for why we won't do something. Linda didn't let her problems stop her and I didn't let mine stop me. Do not give up if you hit obstacles, because you will. We all do.
- √ Don't let not having money to advertise or set up an office stop you.
- √ When you sponsor someone, you are responsible for them. If you don't have the money for advertising, then go out and generate business by following the examples I and many others did. Take those leads and, with the customers who

have experienced success with your product, show them how to earn extra income by giving them some leads to get cash in their pocket right away.

√ Put into them what they are giving to you. Let them know that you believe in them and paint that picture of success for them. KNOW THEIR DREAMS AND GOALS.

# CHAPTER 5

# TAKING THAT FIRST STEP

So I began my path and found a business that I really wanted to work. In the process I wanted to find the fastest path to success that I could. I ***pictured*** breaking all records.

As with any organization, there are the "newbies" and the "veterans". All around me the "veterans" were talking about reaching that mountaintop and how to capture the flag. The path they were teaching to get to the top of that mountain was laid out and they were intent on following a trail that went around and around the mountain in a spiral.

## THINGS WEREN'T ADDING UP

I didn't want to take ten years to get to the top and my gut was screaming at me that this was not the way. I could tell immediately by some of the things they were teaching, that most of them were going to take a while to even get going. For all intents and purposes, their plans included getting new boots for climbing, shiny gadgets and cool matching outfits, which eliminated most of us from getting started, as we couldn't afford activities and products that should have been considered optional, although they were made necessities.Things such as fax and copy machines, computers, fancy letterhead, new desks, just the right pens and so on were taking precedence over just selling the product. Couple that with the fact that their road map included unnecessary rest stops (meetings) to catch their breath every few miles. They were putting on meetings three times a week then they would discuss and have another meeting, go out to dinner to discuss more meetings. They had been in the company 15 years and were teaching that we could achieve their level of success--$10,000 a month and more-- by talking to ten people a day.

On the surface, from an outsider's perspective, it would seem to be a good route. All of this intense and focused preparation eemed very official, but it rang hollow to me. They wanted nothing more than to make me one of them, a "prepper". Yet, all of this preparation without action looked to me as if it would take ten years to find any success. This ran completely against my immediate need to get out of debt. Because of the books I had been reading, I knew there was a better way.

## LESSONS LEARNED AND SHARED

√ So many teach others how to be a plow horse. Work hard all day with your head down, and in ten years, you will be successful. Why not be a racehorse?! Follow a blueprint where you can talk to 10,000 people a day.

√ After charging up $800 of sales on Linda's merchant account, she wouldn't return my calls so I could get paid. Months went by and I was so discouraged I wanted to quit. I called the company to tell them that my upline refused to pay me and they said that I was an independent distributor and I had to work it out on my own. $800 was a lot of money to me, and I almost quit, but I'm glad I didn't. Imagine if I had. I would have lost the life I have now.

# CHAPTER 6

# WHERE'S THE LEVEL PLAYING FIELD?

When I got started in network marketing the environment was the same as it is today. It's difficult to connect with your upline that is making millions. Back then, there were no Skype Groups or online webinars, and information about how to succeed was scarce, so I had to do a lot of digging, in order to find out how and why people in my area were successful, so that I could duplicate their efforts. Unfortunately, I was often met with resistance. This never slowed my ambition.

## WHO'S TRYING TO CAP YOUR AMBITION?

The company I was involved with at the time had already been around 15 years. I lived in Seattle at the time and the area didn't bring in enough sales to warrant a company sponsored training—where was the level playing field in that?

If my sponsor didn't hold training sessions and couldn't be reached I couldn't figure out how I was supposed to grow. None of the people in my local group were as determined and I hadn't seen any one of them as top earners at the national convention.

At the convention I learned that there was one other group 2 hours from me, but still in my area, that was learning marketing skills from one of the highest earners in the company.

After attending the huge annual convention and believing in the familial words that were shared "All of us work together!" I decided to attend his meeting knowing in my heart that everyone in the company was here to help everyone succeed.

At the event, I had been spellbound. Sitting in the last row of the huge center, I was watching the screen, because the people on stage looked like ants. The words of the owner and founder of the company sank deep. "We are your family," he said. "Take a look at the person sitting next to you, that guy or girl is going to be there to help you when you have a bad day. When your family or spouse makes fun of you for trying to reach your dreams you tell them that there are 1.2 million others realizing their dreams that are just waiting to help you."

Getting ready to go to that local training weeks later, I borrowed my mother's blazer and skirt, made a sack lunch because I couldn't afford to eat there. I put my last ten bucks into the gas tank, with the hope and confidence that I would at least learn one thing that would increase my sales. I drove my beat up Honda two hours in the snow on bare tires.

Barely making it on time, I saw the one of the few chairs available, way up in front. I scrambled up the forty or more rows, happy that I would finally be trained. Two good things in a row; I had avoided crashing on the freeway with my bare tires and now I had snagged a seat so close that I would be able to see and hear everything the speaker had to say. I wouldn't miss anything. I was going to learn how to be a millionaire.

***

The energy was electric. Settling in, I could hear all the excited conversations buzzing around me, as well as shouts of "Hey, you look great!" and "It's good to see ya, how are Davy and Jen-jen?" The realization hit; these people knew each other. In fact they knew each other really well.

I chided myself for regressing back into the little kid that hated the little kid who hated to walk into class late. This wasn't like grammar school, with all eyes staring at you and little boys making teasing remarks because you were late. I reminded myself that the company was 15 years old; and of course everyone knew each other. It would be odd if they didn't. Especially with this being the most successful group in town. In fact, I figured, they would probably be clamoring to help me once they found out how my sponsor had essentially abandoned me.

## THE MOMENT I HAD BEEN WAITING FOR

The speaker walked in. A broad grin spread across my face. My favorite speaker from the annual convention was here now; it would all be all right. I knew I was definitely going to learn something tonight. The two hour drive in the snow, with bare tires (worse than bald), my last ten bucks in the gas tank, the borrowed blazer and skirt, it wasn't all for nothing.

I set my lunch bag under my seat. I took out my pens and new notebook, got my water out of my purse. I put everything within arm's reach. I was going be prepared when it came time to ask questions. This was the moment.

The company promised that if I worked hard, became teachable and helped others, I would be up in the seven figures too. This was going to be the man that helped me.

The speaker began, "Before we start... "

I leaned in, concentrating on every word that came out of his mouth. The speaker looked kindly up there under the lights, the platform in front of him, his glasses and slightly balding head shining back at us assuredly. His presence gave off the feeling that if he could make all that money, we could too.

He continued, "Is there anyone here that is not in my organization, but another line?" Almost knocking over my water, I raised my hand excitedly. I thought to myself: this guy is great. He's going to take time to acknowledge those of us who had come all this way that were not even in his group.

I saw another hand go up. I almost fist-pumped the air. My first distributor had also shown up. Bouncing in my chair, thrilled that the snow hadn't stopped him either, I waved. A huge smile lit up my whole face. He waved back from the last row on the other side of the enormous room.

The speaker finished, "I'm sorry, but this is a closed meeting. You will have to leave."

All the color drained from my face. I was stunned. Then it flamed a hot red. A mixture of anger, frustration, and embarrassment flooded my body. Shaking so hard my notebook fell, along with all of my pens. I dived down trying to hide myself under the chair. I couldn't see. Tears blinded me.

As I tried to reach two of my pens, the man behind me kicked them at me. Ink marks stained my mother's light grey suit. I was mortified.

I felt the entire room staring at me, waiting. I could feel that they were annoyed that they were missing valuable teaching minutes, because of me. The two women, on each side of me, shoved my notebook and water bottle into my hands. Their eyes said everything. They didn't want me there. The speaker stood on the platform, microphone silent, refusing to let me hear any millionaire-making tips. I popped up, wiping my eyes, smearing mascara on the only thing I could find, my poor mother's suit sleeve.

## I REALLY AM ON MY OWN

I thought to myself, "Isn't *one* person going to stand up and say something?" These two-hundred people in the room were the top earners in the entire company. Didn't any of them remember their first days as a new distributor? What had happened to the words they had applauded and cheered during the convention? "All of us work together!" they had shouted. It had only been a week since they had heard their beloved Founder tell us that helping each other would get us to $1 billion in sales.

Finally reaching the exit door, I heard a man clear his throat. I turned around, hopeful. Then I saw he was standing with my brown paper bag held high enough for the people in the far back to see.

"You forgot your lunch!" he shouted and tossed it to me. I stepped out into the cold as the laughter rang in the background. Knowing my one distributor was long gone, I bit down on my lower lip, drawing blood. Getting into the freezing car, I dropped the ignition key twice. I finally got the key in the ignition and for once my car turned over on the first try. The speakers came to life and the cassette tape filled the air, the Founder talking directly to me.

"Let me tell you--- I had a lot of things go wrong for me when I first started in the business... but what would have happened if I had quit the first time somebody was mean to me?" Thousands of feet from the live tape started pounding the floors in unison along with cheers, people knowing they wouldn't be there if he had quit. Me knowing I couldn't quit. I grabbed my notebook and pen and wrote: Things I will NEVER do when I am number one. HAVE CLOSED MEETINGS.

**READ MY BLOG ONLINE, WWW.CHRISCARLEY.WORDPRESS.COM**

I have a blog online that is up to date in showing my experiences and the adventures I have had in my life. One master of visualization whom I know personally, and who has been a friend and mentor, is Donald Trump. He taught me that no matter what stage in your life you are in, you need to imagine and speak on the success of things you want to see come to pass. This is an excerpt from my blog detailing when Donald Trump's show, "The Apprentice", first began to air.

**Beach Boy's concert and dinner at Donald Trump's Palm Beach club Mar-a-Lago.**

In my 30's, I not only met Donald, but he became my friend and teacher. One big event where I think Diana

Ross was playing; Donald took the stage and started bragging about having a number one hit TV reality show. He proclaimed, to about 500 of us, that his show The Apprentice was breaking all records. He went on and on and as others around us whispered about his arrogance I grinned my head off. His show hadn't aired yet! He was using the Universal Law Of Attraction. I saw him after the show and congratulated him. We laughed and talked about how powerful words and thoughts are, how whatever we talked about, email about, text and pass forward is what we get, good or bad. Months later, during another celebrity show, Donald got up on stage and said that the coming Friday, The Apprentice was going head to head with the number one show in the world for years: Friends. He told us all that his show was going to stomp that number one hit and be the biggest ratings ever. No one at the enormous table I was sitting at believed it would happen except for me. I knew he was using the Ether (a medium that fills all space and supports the propagation of electromagnetic waves, the fifth and highest element after air, earth, fire and water or the magnetic Intelligence Force (God) that holds our planets in space. Understand how a magnet attracts objects. Look it up. Study it.

**Sure enough, his show was the number one hit, out pulling Friends by a landslide.**

There is no Secret. You've got to put your words out in the direction you want your life to become. The only way to do this in a world filled with so many focusing on the bad things going on, ignoring the wonderful things we all enjoy every day, is to change your thoughts and words to what you would like the world to be. You have to be teachable. You have to study. You have to care about each other and help those who reach out to you.

Donald helped me a lot. I learned so much from him. The people who were and are in my organization who are earning massive amounts of money, followed through with everything I told them to do. They read the books that successful people read every day so when they get around someone who is negative or discouraged, it doesn't bother them. In fact, they are able to make a change in that person's life by being positive and inspiring. I could always see when someone was going to make it because of what they were putting into their minds. I challenge everyone to become the person that does this and reach out for the desires that God put into them and declare that they will fulfill everything that He created you to be. You can do this today by changing every doubt that comes into your mind to a thought of gratefulness and appreciation for what you do have. This is a chance to instill in your subconscious that it doesn't have to take years or months even to start attracting health and happiness into your life and your loved ones. Each time you replace a negative thought with a declaration that you are not mediocre that you have the skills inside you to become great, that you were born with them, that each of you has this power inside of you that you can tap into at any time, everything will come to you. Start by going to your library and checking out the books: Think and Grow Rich (Rich in Spirit, ideas, hope, love) by Napoleon Hill. The magic of Believing and TNT it Rocks the Earth by Claude Bristol and get your kids and grandkids to study them too! I promise you, you will see amazing miracles start happening.

## LESSONS LEARNED AND SHARED

√ Give your mind information that there are millions of people actually making money during our economic times. People all over are taking control of their lives and working for themselves.

- √ We know, as a scientific fact, that the mind controls our body. This means that when you focus on success the body responds accordingly as well.
- √ Start giving your mind information on how to protect you. In just fifteen (15) minutes to half an hour read the books that teach you how to use more of your mind. Program your mind, before you go to sleep, giving it information from the greatest teachers in the world.
- √ Open your mind to ideas and thrilling concepts that will fire your cells up as you sleep, bringing to you better ideas, plans and the energy to find your path.
- √ Wake up thinking about "What You Want". Lay there for ten minutes doing nothing but showing your brain what you want to experience for the day.
- √ Success is not an accident. All the desire, motivation, and determination will not get you there, if you are following the wrong plan.

# CHAPTER

# 7

# MY EPIPHANY

I knew that I wanted to be successful and I decided that I wasn't going to be deterred. My phone was ringing off the hook from cheap, hand-written posters I had put up on telephone poles that said: FREE SAMPLES! Lose up to 30lbs, $30, 30 day guarantee. I took the money I earned from those signs and bought my first ad in my local newspaper. That ad paid for itself, so I kept it there, and even purchased an ad in the city next to it. When that ad paid for itself, I bought ads in newspapers throughout the entire state. The company I was looking at was strong. Analysts and business professionals had them listed as a top company. I loved their product and 95% of the population needed that product. It looked like all conditions were right. Knowing that the top people in the company had been talking to ten people a day for 15 years, I had to find some way to talk to thousands a day to catch up with them. So, I made a tape of me making sales and made a video of me telling my story. I then had my people use these tools so we wouldn't get burned out.

The beauty of those tools was the fact that they could talk to people while we were sleeping and having family time.

## SUCCESS CAN BE FOUND LURKING ANYWHERE

I started reading Think and Grow Rich and all of the books Wayne Dyer had written and put up sticky notes that had $10,000 a month on them all over my apartment. The books all said that we didn't have to know "How" that if we pictured "the end result" we would emit a different vibration that would attract the right people and opportunities to us. As my customers lost weight and I gave them leads and put money in their pockets right away, my organization began to grow and my monthly checks started doubling. I qualified for a top party with the company. I was thrilled. I was going to meet the stars and top millionaires and get a chance to learn how they did it. I arrived early to the champagne event but found it hard to get anyone to talk to me. I found myself leaning against a wall, on the outside. That's when I noticed Bob Anderson standing next to me and I introduced myself. "Hi, I'm new here, made my first cut of President's team ($10,000 royalties) in just my 10th month retailing."

He introduced himself and said: "I just made fully qualified president's team in my 12th month recruiting."

I shared with him how my group was retailing and he invited me to fly in and teach his group and he would teach me how they were recruiting.

He was amazed at the marketing tools I was bringing to the table. He had never used them himself, but he could see the potential.

## NOT EVERYONE IS GOING TO GET IT

As a team, we approached the veterans group; the same veterans group that had set themselves up as "preparation" experts for the past 15 years. Thus far, they had only modest success to show for their efforts. As a gesture of good faith and willingness to collaborate we showed them our new techniques and volunteered to teach it to them.

The thought was simple, "Why don't we take all your great ideas, incorporate these new tools we invented, that were already *tested,* and together build a chair lift and just buzz straight up the side of the mountain and get to the top fast and fun?"

I felt that time was of the essence. The mountain was steep, and there would be some hard days ahead, but all the conditions were perfect; we needed to start NOW. We all had to ask ourselves a hard question. Could the gravy train stop? Who knew when there might be a competing company right behind us? I tried to get them to understand that we couldn't see into the future, we couldn't see around the bends and turns of the route ahead, but right now, today, that flag was obtainable, if we worked together. No packhorses for us, we wanted to run like racehorses.

## NOT EVERYONE WANTS TO BE A RACEHORSE

Well, sadly, the old group of veterans got really mad that we wanted to change things. They really didn't understand that we were giving them a chairlift instead of hiking up the mountain the long way. After thinking that way for so long, no matter how brilliant our plan was, they simply thought we were insane. They were even mad at us for challenging their expertise and not only turned their backs on us, but they told everyone to throw snowballs at us.

They even took it one step further and got some really big, heavy guns, to slow us down; lawyers. Their sole purpose had become to knock us over and bruise us so we couldn't climb, as opposed to selling product and making money.

For the most part, it was really sad, but our tiny group wrapped our arms around each other and took advantage of the new opportunity before us.

## LESSONS LEARNED AND SHARED

√ Help your neighbor and the rewards will come back to you ten-fold. Enough said.

√ *"Why not be a racehorse?'* To this day I hear speakers teaching the theory that your goal to success should be like a packhorse. 'Just stay on the path,' be diligent,' 'this is not a sprint it is a marathon'.

√ You don't have to follow that plan! You can have success now! You can learn and earn at the same time. What you focus on, what you believe and think, is what will happen.

# CHAPTER 8

# TAKING THE MOUNTAIN

I saw right away that any business you decide to go into is like a mountain. 'Success' would be that flag at the top of that mountain. Sometimes, you are going to climb that mountain by yourself, but usually you will have partners, colleagues and seasoned associates that have been in that business, on that mountain, for a while. Franchises are a lot like that, but it also applies to almost any successful business. Real Estate offices, car dealerships, Network Marketers, again almost any businesses you can think of will have someone showing you the 'ropes' or training you.

## NATURE OF SUCCESS

Picture that all of you are at the bottom of a mountain, looking up at the success flag at the faraway peak. Dead bodies of all who haven't made it are strewn about the place. Some are even trampled, stepped on. All of you have the same goal. You and your team want to get to the top.

There are a lot of different ways to reach that top. You could follow the footsteps of the people that have gone before you, but if you learned that it had taken them 10 years, at least to make it just to the halfway point, is that the route you want to go? You could mortgage your home, sell everything you have, take out as many credit cards as you could and buy a vehicle to get you up there. There were sales men everywhere trying to sell you magic hiking boots, a ride on a group bus with special wheels that are on order, even special wings that would allow you to fly up there. Which way is the best way to go?

You have to find a way and a path that fits you and you must be willing to look at the advice you are given for exactly what it is worth. If someone is on a 10 year plan, it may not be for you, particularly if you are on a 2 or 3 year plan.

## LESSONS LEARNED AND SHARED

√ Before you listen to someone and follow the plan they are teaching ASK TO SEE THEIR CHECK and FIND OUT HOW LONG THEY HAVE BEEN IN THE COMPANY.

√ If they aren't willing to show you their check, do NOT follow their plan.

# CHAPTER

# 9

# KNOW YOUR WORTH

As I got through my hurdles and began developing success, others, in and out of my downline, would reach out to me for advice. One such person , we will call her Debbie, was a school teacher, a wonderful lady who I was helping build her new business.

## REAL SUCCESS REQUIRES UNCONVENTIONAL THINKING

Debby had received a phone call from a salesgirl from a local Seattle radio station asking her if she'd be interested in buying "air time." The radio sales rep had seen a small ad of Cindy's that I had given her. "WILLPOWER in a Bottle. Lose weight feel great. FREE SAMPLES! $-back guarantee." It was an ad that had pulled for Cindy right away, but didn't cost her a lot of money to place.

I had her call the rep back and say, "Sure, if you buy my product I might be interested in buying air time." The sales girl agreed, but didn't have the money for Cindy's product. They bartered. Cindy let the sales girl try her product for free and the sales girl got Cindy's product mentioned on air for free on the radio. They got enough sales to pay for more ads and the rep began selling Cindy's product!

## NOT A ONE TIME FLUKE

This kind of bartering, "product for advertising", wasn't just a one-time fluke. A newscaster on one of Seattle's morning show saw a poster that had been put up by another of my team members, who was just starting out. We will call her Alice. Alice was a single mother of two, was living in an apartment in a drug-infested neighborhood, and didn't... have a lot of money to start her business.

We had made up posters that we stapled to telephone poles at major intersections. (Check to see if this is legal in your city.) The reporter flashed on her poster and Alice's phone number was put out on the morning, noon, and nightly news. Her phone rang off the hook. The reporter actually said on television, that she didn't think the product would work. We called her up. We told her it did. The reporter agreed to try her product on air to see if it was what it claimed to be.

The reporter went back on air to say that she would try Alice's product and then get back to viewers in two weeks. Alice's phones went insane. I stopped by her mangy apartment and she was crying. She couldn't handle all the calls for sales! I laughed until I almost started crying and we turned Alice's 15 minutes of fame into over $5,000 a month. I think it was just about four months later I was helping her move out of that horrible apartment into her first home.

## WHERE THERE'S A WILL

Over the year we repeated bartering for ads in

other states as well. Another gal was asked to sponsor her friend in a charity walk-a-thon. She didn't have any money, but she made a deal with her friend to wear her advertising. They actually hand-wrote it on the back of her t-shirt! She would donate a portion of the sales. Her friend was walking in the event anyway, so she agreed. There were thousands of people attending that walk, the news and reporters were there again and they both benefited from the sales that were generated. I have another friend who just bought a valet service for high-end restaurants in Palm Beach. His friend that owns a limo company asked him to hand out his cards to any of the patrons of the restaurants he serviced that might have had too much to drink and needed a driver. He made a deal that he would give out his friends limo card if he would, in return, tell his clients of his Valet service when they had private parties at their million dollar mansions.

## EVERYONE YOU ARE BUYING FROM SHOULD BE BUYING FROM YOU

Think about how often you are approached to buy something. Think about every time you do buy something. Here are some more examples: My one friend barters her product with her maid, the gardener, pool person, hairdresser, nail technician, doorman. She refuses to do business with anyone unless they do business with her. What happens if they don't want your product? Find someone who will! She went through four hairdressers until she found one who would do her hair if she would give her free product.

Be careful about thinking that you don't have a service to barter. I've shown Realtors how to use this concept, and I've shown printers, car salesmen and lawyers; the list goes on and on. Now think about your grandma, your parents, your friends, and your neighbors. Aren't people coming to them to have them buy something?

Isn't just about everyone you know sooner or later going to need to buy a new television, car, house, furniture, or computer? Doesn't just about every one of these businesses involve a sales person? These are just a few ideas to incorporate into generating more for just about whatever business you are in.

## LESSONS LEARNED AND SHARED

- √ My favorite advice to give has always been: "If you treat your business like a million dollar business, it will respond like one!" When in doubt about how to proceed in your marketing, do what the big guys do, follow the business that has the biggest check, (and please don't miss this... ..) *in the shortest amount of time.*
- √ Don't try to copy someone you can't! If someone is teaching you to talk to people one on one, ask them how long they have been in the business. If they tell you 30 years, then copy that person if you want to take 30 years to succeed!
- √ There is always room for improvement on any tools. There is nothing wrong with coming up with a great new idea that you think is even better than the one making you millions a year. Just use the same rule as all these big companies do: TEST IT BEFORE YOU RELEASE IT. ADD TO YOUR MOMENTUM, DON'T STOP THAT MONEY MAKING MACHINE. KEEP IT GOING WHILE YOU TEST A NEW ONE.

# CHAPTER 10

# WHERE ARE THEY NOW?

As I mentioned early on in my network marketing life, two different groups turned their backs on me. One attempted to humiliate me, the others ignored me at first, then went against me. It's probably happened to you in some form or another as well. Even with well-meaning friends attempting to give you unsolicited advice.

I combined what Bob Anderson was doing that was achieving fast results with my ideas and we both got a rocket ride to the top. From all the books I studied on marketing and advertising and 'how to' sell, I taught his group how to retail, get upgrades, massive referrals, and turn their leads into a customer with the company for life.

## GIFT HORSE SABOTAGE

I experienced more pain from the other groups trying to hold me back than I did going straight up that mountain! That's okay. I brought just six of my salespeople with me and from that six, created an income of over $100,000 a month in about 14 months of incorporating our materials, which did all of the work for us. That chairlift really did turn into a rocket and because the other group was still on the mountain spending most of their times flinging snowballs at us, they didn't get a rocket of their own!

## TEN MORE YEARS OF PREPARATION

Ten years after my success, I decided to do a little check up on my old "veteran" friends. I found out that many of them were sadly in the same place. In fact, the entire group had still not made it, and they had actually lost some people along the way. Basically many of the so-called "veterans" had fallen and rolled back down the mountain. Some had even been pushed back down by their own partners that were climbing next to them!

## THE SILVER LINING

Do I feel vindicated? Heck no. I truly wanted to be part of that group that had been around me early on. They say it's lonely at the top. For me it was. I felt a void in the vacations I took and the parties I attended. All the while I just kept following my marketing rules and making money. Eventually the veterans group and I made amends. I called them up one day to share my marketing blueprint. In fact I encouraged them to copy it, and they finally did.

# CHALLENGE

# 1

# 28 Day Challenge to Blossom Your Ambition

I read a statistic somewhere that we spend an average of five years in the bathroom during our lifetime. Make use of that time. Have books in your bathroom! For anyone that wishes someone would help them achieve a better life, that is reading this right now, whether you believe what I am telling you or not; if you would commit to simply doing the following habits for 28 days, your life will change forever.

Your. Life. Will. Change. Forever. Do you understand? It doesn't matter if you believe me or not. Just like going to the gym every day for 28 days and doing exactly what your trainer tells you to, your life will change forever. Even if you don't ever work out again, you will keep some of what you learned, your cells have memory, and your muscles have memory, until you leave your body.

I throw this challenge out to everyone. This is for millions of people that say that they want to stop working frantically, stressfully, and want to stop putting in 70 hour weeks.

I have NEVER had someone tell me that they followed through with all the steps and didn't reach any of their goals. NEVER. I have had couples and individuals unfortunately stop after the 28 days and a year or two later they are back where they started, sometimes even worse off.

These daily habits are as important as drinking water. If you stop, and you go back to focusing on what is wrong in our society and world then your thoughts send a different signal to your cells and they in turn wear you out.

Attract more of whatever you are focusing on, sending a picture to your brain so that your thoughts bring you whatever you are constantly putting in front of it. Why not be the ½ of %1 that enjoy life, have the excitement and the energy to life it to its fullest and for the next 28 days incorporate the following plan into your life.

## DO THIS PLAN FOR JUST 28 DAYS

1. Stop watching television or nonsense YOUTUBE. Don't be afraid that you are going to miss something important there will always be people around you to tell you about all the gloom and doom. Before you go to bed watch, listen to, or read something motivational. Whatever your mode of learning is. If your spouse complains, go into another room, or put earphones on.
2. When you wake up and before you open your eyes, picture and think about the entire day going great and see yourself where you want to be next

month, next three months, and go into great detail. See the new car you are driving, see your family where you want them to be, see yourself, wearing the kind of clothes you've always wanted, the office you've dreamed about or the vacation you've always wanted.

3. Listen to something motivational, such as a CD or MP3, while you are getting ready, fixing breakfast, driving to work. If your family isn't willing to help you, see them sitting around the breakfast table listening and talking about the CD that will change their future.

4. As they start to see you change, actually witness you becoming happier, healthier, and see the amazing effects it can't help but rub off on them. They will decide as a family to give this a try for just 28 days. When this happens you will see something phenomenal happen. As the people around you become involved, you now have even more energy in your household. Energy of excitement, success, and now as you have more minds working together, you become more powerful, success comes faster.

5. Wherever you are during the day, take a break and refuel. Just like you need to eat your lunch to feed your body and brain, you will need to refuel your mind. Maybe you were in a meeting where everything was negative, or you let your co-worker talk for hours about everything bad in her life, or you even joined in and told her stories about how bad your life was. STOP. Say, "Let's talk about what is good in our life." Focus on the fact that you have two arms and two legs. Focus on the fact that you are now reading this book, that

you can see and even though you have a job that you don't like, you do have a job. If you don't, then look for anything that you are thankful for. If it isn't much, then start talking about what you want to have. Talk in detail about the perfect spouse you want, the career or business you want to have. FILL YOUR MIND WITH ANYTING AND EVERYTHING THAT MAKES YOU FEEL GOOD.

# *Action…*

*We have proven that space and time are not conditions in which we live; they are modes in which we think. What we see depends upon the theories we use to interpret our observations.*

*~Note from Albert Einstein's diary*

# CHAPTER 11

# MY FIRST SUCCESSFUL BUSINESS

As a child I was always coming up with ways to make money. As you have already read I also really learned about network marketing by selling walnuts and getting others enrolled in my success. As I grew older the entrepreneurial spirit never left me, but like all young people I had multiple odd jobs in order to make ends meet. One such odd job was being a waitress. Unlike most though, I didn't approach being a waitress really as a job. I saw it as a business.

## OPERATING MY WAITRESS BUSINESS

Being a waitress was the first business I was involved in that I became a success. There are millions of waitresses and waiters around the world. Oftentimes they are taken for granted. They are the invisible workforce that day in and day out interacts with customers intimately.

Yet, few people really stop to ask themselves "What is a waitress?"

The answer is simple. They are service people. If they are really good and effective, they are ultimately the key to a restaurant operating at 100%. They are the restaurant's "salespeople."

Few people really understand the restaurant business. They come in, look at the menu and think they ordered what they wanted, have their meal and leave. This is far from the truth. Behind the scenes there are quotas for wait staff (i.e. sales force), there are contests for pushing different items, management will tell the wait staff what items need to be sold immediately, and the value of every plate of food is known down to the penny. Don't forget the tip. This is just one form of the total "commissions" that go back to the "sales force", better known as the ""wait staff".

So as a waitress my eyes were opened to the inner workings of this mechanism. I quickly realized that my job was a business, that I had an opportunity to make as much as I want, within reason of course, if I approached this with my focus on the customer.

## THE ONION RING LOAF CONTEST

One month I was there, we had a contest going on who could sell the most onion ring loaf appetizers. The restaurant I was working for did these promotions often and was always keen on giving recognition to successful service people, in addition to handing out bonuses. This made me excited and kicked in the competitive side of me instantly. At the same time the restaurant had somehow gotten a great deal on a white wine as well. So the contest rules were simple, who ever could sell the most appetizers got a bottle of wine and a free dinner.

This was a win/win for the restaurant. They moved more onion ring loaf appetizers and the "bonus" that they gave us, the white wine, was something that they were receiving at less than wholesale prices anyway and the dinner was at cost.

In this month long contest I won almost every single night, following a very simple formula that can and should be implemented in every business. I later applied the exact same formula to another contest at the restaurant, and eventually used much of it to become a successful in network marketing.

## MY WAITRESS BUSINESS FORMULA

When my customer was seated, I "recognized" them with a friendly greeting, then "planted a seed", "limited their choices", "gave them a testimonial", and "created urgency", all in the span on 1-2 minutes .

Example:

I greeted them, found something positive to say about how they looked, their children etc. *(recognition)*

I then told them in great detail how our number one appetizer and wine 'special' was incredible. *(planted a seed) (limited choices)*

I used basic sales and advertising phrases of 'everyone'. *(testimonial)*

"One of our most popular appetizers. Everyone that tried it loves it. Sometimes we even run out." That last phrase I also learned upped my sales. (created urgency)

## KEEP YOUR INTEGRITY

Now mind you these phrases were all true, but they really could have been applied to any of our appetizers. There were at least six or seven other appetizers for them to choose from, and they were all very good and popular.

Yet, I could see that the customers almost always went with the wine or appetizer that I suggested, because of the formula I was using. Everyday that I won this little contest I also gained more confidence.

I was a new employee and didn't get the same respect the other employees had earned from being there so long. It was the only leveling tool that let me be noticed by the manager and the owners. As a result of this contest, and many more, I ended up being assigned to the best shifts. I essentially got to pick my own hours and the most important part, I became recognized by my peers as a wonderful waitress. The same "recognition" that I was giving, was now being given to me. It felt really good to come into work each night.

My tips (commissions) were higher than everyone else, every single night I worked. I was then tasked with teaching the other wait staff the technique above. As a result the whole restaurant made more money and the top wait staff began to really help and include me.

## LESSONS LEARNED AND SHARED

√ No matter where you are in life you can apply "basic marketing strategies".

√ Remember you are always selling. You sell yourself to your boss, your spouse, children so develop these skills.

√ Read books on marketing and advertising. If you just learn one tiny thing your business and your life will explode.

√ Pay attention to advertising that is mailed to your home. I ordered a swim suit from Victoria's Secret 20 years ago and I still get a catalog in my mail.

√ Think about what gets you to buy something. Incorporate that into what you are doing.

√ When you add FREE SAMPLES and Money back guarantee to your adveristing or business cards you will pull much more.

# CHAPTER 12

# COPYING THE SUCCESS BLUEPRINT

I still smile when I think of the first time my dad saw my mansion in Malibu. The man who had lent me $79 to begin my journey in network marketing was finally going to see what his seed had sown.

My dad, a factory worker for Boeing his entire working life, looked around in amazement, just watching the majestic gates rolling open. I clearly remember him and my mom climbing up to enter the house. Zuma beach was sparkling brightly in the background. I saw his eyes dart across the 3 acres. Taking in the putting green, sand trap, the two-story artist's cottage, a guest house, and finally the main house. He blurted out, "Are you sure you can afford this?"

Mom told me that night, "Your Dad freaked out when we pulled in and begged me to stop pretending, thinking I had the driver pull in to someone else's place!" She was talking fast, waving her arms in the air, mimicking Dad shaking his head, eyes narrowed, his familiar features stating, *'I don't believe you.'*

My dad and grandfathers are gone now, but their values aren't. The work ethic, the drive, and the unwavering belief if you are "paid a dollar, you work a dollar" have been instilled in me. I applied all of those same ethics into my success blueprint to make network marketing work for me. Most importantly I focused on not reinventing the wheel completely, just perfecting the success blueprint for my industry.

## WORK SMARTER, NOT HARDER

As a kid, whenever we drove past million-dollar homes, I wondered how all those people had gotten so successful. Why them and not us? My father told me that 'those people' had two and even three homes just as magnificent.

I wanted to jump out of the car and run up and ring their doorbell and ask them how they became so wealthy. Were they smarter than us? Luckier? Did they work harder? Had all of them inherited their money? Finally, at age 33, and after working I figured it out: *They just knew more than I did.*

It made sense to me, that if I could learn how they had become so successful and applied those same principals, I could do the same. It's no secret that throughout the ages, success blueprints have been left behind for anyone that sincerely seeks them. These success blueprints sit around freely.

Behind every billion-dollar company there is first a start-up, and all any of us have to do, to achieve the same success is: *Copy Success*.

## GOOD MARKETING IS FOR EVERYONE

No matter what profession, job, career, or position you have right now in your life, your first step in getting where you want to go is to learn how to deliberately market yourself. Waitresses, doctors, lawyers, managers, house cleaners, actresses, singers, executives—even Owners of large and small corporations all have to deliberately use the marketing skills that they have relied on naturally. Only if, and this is a big if, they desire an increase in income and business.

In any situation, place or position, you find yourself today, learning how to market yourself will change your future and your present by applying it now.

Copy and run your business (or job) exactly like the billion-dollar companies that make the products you buy every day. When you emulate them you will achieve the same, if not better results. There is a proven science behind their success, use it. Microsoft, Dell, McDonald's, you name it, you can give yourself a competitive advantage that no one else has when you religiously follow their examples. All successful companies and any business you can think of, all use the same success blueprint when they start up, as they take off, and continue using this same success blueprint for decades for one reason only, *it works.*

When the blueprint is ignored, people lose money, miss promotions, salary increases, opportunities, and repeat business. Oftentimes instead of copying what has already *proven* to work they want to go off on their own, leaving the success blueprint behind. This is a tragedy. It means that they never get going or they go into debt trying to get started, thus losing their life's dream, whatever it may be.

## DEVELOPING THE SUCCESS BLUEPRINT

It is unfortunate how neglected the library is these days. With the explosion of the internet, library hours have been cut around the nation. In ancient times libraries were revered. Not just anyone could enter the "Temple of Knowledge" and check out the scrolls. Today, at most, you may need a state ID and they will give you a free card to check out as many books as you want, until your heart's content. Yet still people don't patronize them like they should.

Starting out I didn't have the money to buy motivational tapes, books, or movies. The library was my only refuge. As it can be, for anyone, that desires more from their lives. When you cannot afford to go to a bookstore and pay for every book that you want or need, the library is there to give you the wisdom you need to get you through the tough times.Whether you buy the books or you check them out from the library, as you begin to study motivators and successful people you begin to see that there is clearly a success blueprint at play. Luck can only account for a small fraction of their success, particularly when that success has been sustained for decades.

## TAPPING INTO THE SUCCESS BLUEPRINT

Every successful person I have ever met, especially Donald Trump, whom I got to know well, utilizes a success blueprint daily. As part of manifesting my own "success blueprint", I was the only single female under 40 to join both of Donald Trumps exclusive clubs in Palm Beach. In fact he went out of his way to welcome me and every chance he got, he would introduce me to famous people. At that time, he was my mentor, and he was so much fun. This only manifested because of my self-belief.

Success always begins first with an unwavering self-belief. If you have ever seen or heard Donald Trump interviewed, he constantly lets everyone know, "I am The Greatest," and "My product is the best".

Muhammad Ali was notorious for incorporating this as part of his success blueprint. Politicians utilize this in their success blueprint. Oprah goes about it wonderfully. The reality of the success blueprint is that you must first successfully market yourself, to yourself. When you can do that, others will also believe in what you are selling. Unwaveringly, you must understand that at all times you are marketing yourself. If you don't believe you, then who will?

You do not need to be vocal when first incorporating this into your success blueprint, keep in mind though, Muhammad Ali and Donald Trump first started vocally using this component of the success blueprint before they became visibly successful. It's likely that had they not already incorporated their self-marketing, they never would have gotten to where they are today.

Part of self-marketing required them to visualize what they wanted their end result to be. Then they focused on it hourly, daily, to reinforce their success blueprint.

I'll guarantee you that when Donald sets out to open a new multi-billion dollar show, or a new golf course, he first 'sees it' in his mind's eye. He talks about it constantly. He puts his thoughts down on paper, then to a model. He is already convinced of the success of whatever he is promoting, long before he brings anyone else in.

This part of the success blueprint alone will do wonders for you. It's what brought me from the darkest points in my life to my greatest moments of triumph. If you have been doing the "28 Day Challenge", you are already feeling the effects of the power of this part of the success blueprint, through visualization.

## WHAT MY SUCCESS BLUEPRINT PRINICPLES ARE

Now, while the first step in my success blueprint requires unwavering belief in yourself and your product, there are six (6) other key principles to round it out. All seven (7) of these principles combined are how I made millions in network marketing. Many of you will look at the list of the 7 principles of the success blueprint aand will say "huh?" and scratch your head, but a few of you will get the principles upon first glance and run with it. However you react, it will be natural for you to say to yourself, "it can't be that easy."

So what I suggest to you is that you highlight, bookmark, or underline this page. Refer back to this page as often as you like. These principles will give you a clear path to success no matter whatever business you own.

## 7 SUCCESS BLUEPRINT PRINCIPLES

1. Have a great product that you wholly believe in, even if your product is just yourself
2. Use a personal touch to make sure the customer feels like s/he comes first
3. Offer a guarantee
4. Provide good service
5. Pay your customers for referrals
6. Advertise a low cost product and have an upgrade ready

7. Keep track of your buyers and offer incentives to keep them coming back.

## LESSONS LEARNED AND SHARED

√ As you build an organization or sales force, the most important thing you can do for them is to get money in their pocket in their first 4 days. They already have an incredible start because of their emotional high for your product. Reinforce that.

√ My sponsor gave me leads that made me money that day. When I had a customer who had lost weight and experienced better health, I would call them and talk to them about making money off their results. If they weren't interested I added them onto my monthly newsletter where they could see each month how others just like them were growing. As the checks went up each month and the health stories of children, mothers and families were featured I'd get 10-20 calls the week they got the update. They either wanted to register with me or they wanted more products. I'd send out a copy of the newsletter to all my organization and they would add a personal touch and mail it to every person they ever contacted or ran into that had an interest in making more money, working from home or greater health.

√ My people still do that newsletter today and it works. Before company rules prohibited contacting downline underneath a top person, I also mailed it to everyone who shows up on the organization chart the company sends me. I also encourage my subscribers to reach out to me *if they need any help or have any questions and want the kind of checks we are getting please call me.*

√ Over the years, hundreds of people who have signed up, but were lost on what to do, called me. My policy is thatno matter where they are in my line—even if I don't get paid on them, I workwith them.

√ The books I had been reading on Law of Attraction and the Bible taught about giving back and helping all. If I hadn't helped Bob Anderson, he might not have helped me by encouraging me to write the 14 page mailer that allowed me to break all records in the company a year after we started using it.

√ From a 'HowTo' book on advertising I learned I needed to track my stats so I could see what was working and what wasn't. If you miss this step, you will lose millions. Many times when I saw that a stat from one of my people was bad, I immediately called the upline and got on the phone with the person who wasn't doing as well as everyone else. Invariably, they had changed the ad, left out "FREE SAMPLES! Money-back guarantee." Other times, when the ad was exact, I checked their voicemail and it was awful.

√ Nowadays I can record the voicemail for them and each package of information has me on video, audio, and another book, all telling my story. So that by the time the person went through the whole package they would call whoever had sent it to them and say: "I'm in!" This catapulted all our incomes and took away the biggest reason why people fail… NO rejection. If the person had read and watched everything and they weren't interested they mailed it back for a refund. We made people who wanted to start their own business go through 3 steps of elimination and the materials allowed us to talk to millions of people a month while we were sleeping, having fun and working.

√ Now with the internet you can do this easily. You can buy lists of people that want your product—whatever it is—and send them something that entices them to call and order.

# CHAPTER 13

# WHERE DO YOU GET THE CUSTOMERS

A person in the same business as I was in, was trying to get me to buy a 'system' he had developed that he had been promoting to everyone as the reason his check was $70,000 a month after only 3 years in the business. I hadn't made my millions yet and was desperately in search of answer. Without a doubt I was quite impressed with his check so I paid around $1,000 to come to his seminar.

In the seminar all he did was go on and on about how we should now buy his training books, CD's and DVD's. He spent about an hour teaching us how to manage a big team and how to keep motivated. I was devastated when on the lunch break I overheard someone say that they had known him when he was in company X ten years ago. He had been in the industry over 30 years and had taken all the old company's entire sales force over to our company when the old one got into some kind of trouble. I was furious!

There was no way I could duplicate that! No wonder he wasn't able to give any of us any 'meat' to do our business. He had gotten in at the beginning of a company and was in the right place at the right time.

Upon further investigation, I found out that he was making $70,000 a month all right, but it was money made from selling his books and CD's NOT from being successful in the business we all had come to be trained on. Losing a thousand dollars was a lot for me at that time. It almost made me quit!

I went back after lunch and for the next three hours listened to his stories about how great having money was, how unbelievable it was to be able to go on exotic vacations and I sat there shaking my head as he put picture after picture of his new homes, cars and even made his wife stand up and show her diamonds she was wearing!

After another hour of him telling us we needed to have a dream and go out and bring as many people as we could to his next 'training' I couldn't take it and I raised my hand. He seemed to be glad at the interruption and called on me immediately. "I'm really new at this and I am wondering how you got your first people into your business?"

He answered, "I had them buy the product."

I asked again, "How did you find those people that bought your product?"

He smiled and answered as if I were a child. "I had them come to a meeting and then sold it to them."

Now he was trying to get away from me and even though I was embarrassed I just couldn't shut up. "How did you get them to the meeting? Were these people you knew, did you run an ad, what did the ad say, how did you afford to buy an ad if you were just starting out, how did you get these people to show up at your meeting?"

Obviously, I and everyone else had tried to get people to come and hear about our business and buy our product and anyone who has ever done this knows how difficult it is to ask someone to come, let alone to actually have them show up.

He didn't look very happy now, but he said, "There are many ways to do this, you just have to decide that you are going to be committed and go out and do it."

Even though I knew I was being obnoxious, I still couldn't stop. I really wanted to know, I really wanted to succeed. "HOW did you do it?"

Now he was defensive. "I worked my tail off. I talked to everyone I knew and I just kept at it."

I was willing to do that. "What did you say to them? What if you don't really know anyone and your friends and family won't listen to you? Did you just walk up to strangers?" Luckily all the people in the room needed and wanted the same answers and they started to back me up, murmuring, "Why don't you answer her questions?

## SUCCESS DOESN'T HAVE TO BE HARD

We have all seen it. A fly will hit into a glass pane in front of it for hours. He will hit that same glass pane over and over again, when there is an open window or open door nearby.

That poor fly is working really, really hard to get out. He will hit it harder. He will rest or knock himself out, fall to the windowsill and maybe get up again and try. Sometimes he will die trying. If only he would sit back, feel the air coming through, look around and for hardly any effort, any work at all, he could fly through the open window or open door. It was always there. It was always easy. He just didn't see it. He just didn't know about it.

Most people I know who fail in their career, failed, like that fly, because they did not have the knowledge to use that open window, which is our case is advertising, and the steps that follow it. Most of us work hard. Some of us even put in 12-14 hour days to try to make a career and/or business work. We put everything we have into making a success of our venture. Unfortunately, if you are working hard on the things that don't work, you end up failing.

That's why so called gurus, oftentimes do more harm than good. They rarely give concrete help in stopping us from hitting the glass pane. In fact they actually box us in and drive us to despair if we are not careful.

## ATTRACTING CUSTOMERS

What else do you look for or what else gets you to try something? How about when you are at a Costco or your local grocery? What about something that offers you a way that you know you won't get ripped off? What is that one thing that gets you into that business person's "showroom"? It gets you to at least try the product? The magic of the "FREE SAMPLE".

No one in the entire company of millions of salespeople was using this in their ads. The few that had attempted it, couldn't apply it to their business correctly. It was one of the biggest reasons I was able to break all records in just a few yearsof a 15 year old company.

You have to do this right, though, or you can lose a lot of money. I remember being really afraid to do this as each sample cost me 50 cents back then. Now it is funny to think that I was so broke and desperate that 50 cents was a big deal to me, but you have to do exactly like I did or it really ads up if you are on a small or even no-budget.

The free sample can even extend to intangible goods. AOL built their entire business on offering one free month of internet service if you signed up NOW. The beauty of the "free sample" strategy is that it's easy to share by word of mouth. In fact when someone tells you about their business, tell them about your free sample or your free offer. It costs you nothing.

# CHAPTER 14

# UNDERSTANDING AD BASICS

A lot of people think I am a great salesperson, and that is the only reason I have been successful. This is far from the truth. The cornerstone of my approach has been and will always be to follow the successful people. As long as I emulate how the major billion-dollar companies do it, I have to succeed. They have already spent the millions of dollars necessary to study, analyze, and test what works, and what doesn't.

People also believe that because I teach these methods I am somehow immune to their influence. That is far from the truth. It's been said that the best salesmen in the world are the easiest to be sold. On two different occasions advertising basics were used on me, with my full consent, and I ended up succumbing to them, just like anyone else.

## MERCEDES KNOWS HOW TO SELL

Some great examples of this are Mercedes commercials. They usually advertise the car that the largest number of consumers can afford to buy. They show the bottom line price on TV. You will usually see an asterisk along that price, where it says in small print "Does not include upgrades."

When you go into the Mercedes showroom, what happens? You automatically see the most incredible, beautiful most expensive cars they have. The ad that lured me in was for a Mercedes car that cost around $35,000. It interested me and I decided to 'check it out'.

Do this for yourself. Ask to see that car and experience that the sales person will usually tell you that 'this is the one just like it, except that it has a GPS, State of the Art stereo system, dual heat controls, leather interior, hand stitching, neat new phone system.' The car even smells different, when you insist on seeing the car they advertised and compare the two!

The dealership I went to had the advertised car way out back and they forced me to walk through the showroom! Brilliant, by the way. Needless to say, all of these subtle little things wore me down and I bought the most expensive car—about $225,000 I think-- in the showroom with every single gadget I could get.

## THE PORSCHE GUYS MUST KNOW THE MERCEDES GUYS

Years later, I did the same thing at Porsche. I was just going in to buy a second car. There was an ad on television that said you could be in a Porsche for $999/month. This was a far cry from my factory worker days, when I was fretting over .50 cent samples. So I told myself, I'll just look, for the thrill of it.

By no means was I serious about buying, but *the ad drew me in to look*. Steps from the dealership's front doorway, I saw a bright yellow Turbo Carrera with stunning red seat belts and incredible cool gadgets. It was so beautiful, sexy, fun. The Porsche Boxer they had been advertising was again way in the back. Itlooked sad after seeing that gorgeous Carrera. I bought the Carrera that day.

I got pulled over all the time for speeding in Palm Beach and each time the police officer asked me what I was doing wrong I replied: I'm driving a bright yellow $300,000 car." They laughed and let me off with a warning.

## THREE STRIKES YOU ARE OUT

Now that I think of it, the same thing happened with my realtor! I called on a house she had up on the Internet that was around a million dollars. I told her I didn't want to see anything over a million dollars as this was a second home. Over the phone she didn't push me, didn't tell me that houses on the water out in the Florida area I was looking at were running closer to $2 million.

You can probably already see that the same techniques were applied. She showed me those million dollar homes and then she offered to show me one more house that was perfect for me, but a little more expensive.

Before I had called her, I called two other real estate agents. When I told them I wanted to buy a house on the water for no more than a million dollars they didn't know basic marketing techniques and told me that it was impossible. So I went on to find a different agent.

Those two agents lost out on a commission for a two million dollar house that took less than an hour's work. I see this in my industry all the time.

The same thing happens in network marketing. For some strange reason they teach people to sell a $200 product. Out of 10 people, the stats show, only 2 will buy. If you sell a lead in product through FREE SAMPLES at around $30 (this amount has been tested!) and give them samples of your other products that you know they need, you will get 8 out of 10 people that buy, will upgrade, give referrals and come into your business.

I bought the house that day for $1,895,000. No wonder she had been able to advertise herself as one of the top agents. *She followed the basic rules.* If she had tried to tell me over the phone, before she met me, before she established a rapport, I wouldn't have listened. I maybe would have been scared off and *not even met with her.*

## THE THREE BASICS OFADVERTISING

1.) Advertise *FREE items.*

2.) Advertise to get "Your foot in the door"

3.) Advertise to get "Upgrades and Referrals"

If I had known just those three advertising tips alone when I first started, I would have grown even faster than I did. I do not guarantee this book will make you successful. It can help you though by teaching you the tools and fundamentals of marketing and advertising, but you have to apply them. The best advice I have ever received was about how to judge whose advice, training, or guidance I should follow. Look at the check of the person giving the advice and how long they have been in the company.

Don't get sidetracked with anyone who cannot prove what they are telling you! COPY what successful companies and corporations do! Why? Because they are successful and they have ALREADY TESTED IT! The little guy (me, you, any start-up, company or person) has the excitement, drive and will to succeed in their endeavor—or else they would be working for someone else and not reading this book-- but they usually don't have a lot of money to burn and have to get things right or they go broke. COPY what the biggest most successful business has already proven, instead of taking a risk!

McDonalds, Mercedes, Coca Cola, Dell, Sprint, Microsoft... really take a good look at the advertising that is successful. (*You will know that it is successful if the company and the ad is around still).* Smart business people and companies always keep the ad going if it is working. They might test a new ad or idea, but they NEVER STOP an ad, slogan or idea if it is working.

IT IS WORKING if the ad pays for itself.

## ONE EXCEPTION TO THE AD PAYING FOR ITSELF... IMMEDIATELY

An ad might not pay for itself upfront, so be smart and if the initial sale brought you back-end sales, upgrades and referrals, it did pay for itself. Those companies all do something in common that is brilliant and that you should copy. Please pay attention here because this is the number one point that I see almost every single new business, especially MLM people make.

## ADVERTISING THE FREE STUFF

Offer something free. What do you see, almost always, at every major make-up counter in the high-end stores? Revlon, Clinique, Estee Lauder, Lancôme... *Free* make over. Sales girls in the aisles with *'free samples'* of lotion, perfume, aftershave they squirt on you as you try to get by! They are trying to get their foot in the door.

They are trying to get you to stop and sit down. That's all you want as a business owner; to get their attention and to get them to listen. Now, imagine that, after the saleslady squirts you, she tries to sell you $200 worth of products. Compare that to the salesperson who knows basic marketing. She gives you a free half hour make over where she/he will then pamper you, give you attention and explain the targeted products to you and gets you so excited that you just have to have them and you don't even blink when the cashier rings up $200 because you picked out those suggested targeted products, and the sales person *taught you the value of them!* What if she/he went one step further and told you that everyone would be asking why your skin, makeup, hair, etc., looks so good and that you could earn something FREE if you told them about the sales lady that helped you.

## ADVERTISING TO GET YOUR FOOT IN THE DOOR

Advertise and open with your lowest price and with the product that the customer feels or experiences instantly *after* you establish a relationship and you already have their e-mail, address, phone, family history. Then listen to their needs so you can UPGRADE by giving them samples that fulfill that need. Successful companies *advertise* their lowest, most affordable, easiest to understand product *to get you into the door.*

## ADVERTISE TO UPGRADE

When they get you into the showroom, store, home or office or you call them on the phone, or go online and/

or IN THE DOOR, they do everything they can to upgrade you, sell you more, get your address, ask for your phone number, e-mail address. Copy this!

## ADVERTISE TO GET REFERRALS

Copy also that they will give you incentives for anyone you know who wants to buy, giving you a referral compensation for phone numbers, address, e-mail addresses. What happens if you don't buy? You will be put on a mailing list and sent enticements on special offers of products that you showed interest in. A postcard showing their great rates, a grand opening of their dealership, or a sale that is going on. These are all top sales techniques that you should be using in any business you are in.

## LESSSONS LEARNED AND SHARED

√ Every detail adds up. If you don't utilize Basic Marketing Strategies your organization won't either and you will be leaving money on the table every day.

√ Always remember that everything you do is training your person to do. If you don't make this easy, simple and fun—let the materials do the work for you and your salesforce—then they won't be able to duplicate you and will burn out.

CHAPTER

# 15

# ADDITONAL ADVERTISING POINTERS

I remind my students and network marketing partners, there is no honor in suffering. Refuse to hold yourself to the need to take the slow road to success. Don't get caught up in the 'tortoise and the hare' story. The only thing the hare did wrong was take a nap before he crossed the finish line!

Let me repeat myself a little here. I hope to change you and turn everything you have ever heard about the relationship between marketing, sales and advertising upside down. They are interrelated and all are necessary for starting your own business. When done right, one flows into the other.

Not using these proven techniques is the single most common reason I see people acting like the fly, wasting their time banging against a window pane, with an open door a few feet away. They are working so hard. They are putting in long hours. They just refuse to step back and see what the other flies are doing to make it outside!

*Insanity is doing the same thing over and over and expecting a different result.* I read that somewhere and understood it immediately. When you are doing the right thing, it works, when you are doing the wrong thing, it can be disastrous.

## PLEASE TRUST MY KNOWLEDGE

To this very day, even after I have shown hundreds of people how to work smart, some refuse to listen. I even went to extreme measures, providing them with confirmation of my success by showing myself floating in a pool, riding horses and riding my jet ski, even as I accomplished not even ten times more, but hundreds of times more in a tenth of the time they are doing it. After decades, I see them still doing the same thing and so many people still haven't learned.

## ADDITIONAL AD SECRET #1: CREATE A SENSE OF URGENCY

Most retail stores will advertise a 'special' sale, 'One-Day Only'. Labor Day, President's Day, after Thanksgiving Day. Why? Because it works. It creates a sense of urgency. It makes them have to do something very important: "Act Now." They have to follow through or they will lose. The consumer believes they might lose out or the opportunity will be given to someone else. Copy that! It is a proven method that *works.*

## ADDITONAL AD SECRET #2: OFFER MONEY BACK GUARANTEE

In this day and age most of us will not buy anything

that is not guaranteed. If you cannot guarantee your service and product, you should not be selling it. Get involved with something you love. Sell something you truly believe in.

## ADDITIONAL AD SECRET #3: RECOGNIZE YOU'RE EVERYONE

Every statistic about how "recognition" works tells us something very important. Scientists have distilled it down to three reasons why people do the things they do; love, money, and recognition. What do you think is first?

If you guessed that love or money was first, you were wrong; just like me. Recognition is the number one reason people do the things they do. Remember this, study this, and understand that people want to know that they matter. They want service. They want care. Recognition can come in awards, bonuses, gifts even just simple praise, or a 'thank you' card. When I didn't have the cash to pay out promotions I gave them something that would put back into their business. I gave my downline the extra leads I had, the leads I had generated with just a few dollars—posters. FREE SAMPLES! Lose weight feel great, $-back guarantee.

Yesterday I saw a poster that was in the ground by an intersection that read: Massage. First half hour free. Brilliant! I also saw and called on: Hard working housecleaner. We pay for referrals.

My first promotion for my newly sponsored people was that if they listened to a tape on sales and could answer my questions and went to a training seminar they would get three leads.

Then, if they could sell two of those leads our $30

product, they could have five more. My sales force came from my retailing efforts of just getting them to buy one of my least expensive products and then once they felt good about that product (usually only about 4 days) I followed up with them and sold them more and upgraded them and they were already trained.

I had made it so simple that all they had to do was what I did. Sell one product with a free sample, money back guarantee for $30.00, and upgrade them after 4 days. They were also taught to get the new customers information, plant a seed that if they knew anyone that also would like this product they could get a discount or cash reward. That first month in business I sent out a hand-written, cut and paste newsletter. I recognized my customers; printing their words of praise for my great product and I recognized the three customers that had been smart enough to save money and even make money by giving me referrals.

I mailed it out to anyone that hadn't bought, my friends and family and everyone that did buy. Less than 20 people. I doubled my sales with that newsletter and got two more customers that wanted to give me referrals. I even remember them asking if they would be featured in my next newsletter...

## ADDITIONAL AD SECRET #4: FOLLOW UP

Statistics have shown that people need to see/hear things 3-5 times before they buy. You can do a cheap post card, newsletter, and automatic emails . Follow up is also *more* advertising. You see it over and over and you finally start to look at it, *believe* in it. Pepsi, Coke, Sprint phone company, AT&T have been around forever. Why are they still paying for commercials, billboards, and mailings into your homes if they are already so well known? *Because it works.*

## ADDITIONAL AD SECRET #5: TESTIMONIALS.

Really look at the successful advertising. Who do you see on Subway's advertising over and over? Weight-loss commercials, car commercials, and any ad you can think of? They all show satisfied customers with believable testimonies.

## ADDITIONAL AD SECRET #6: FOCUSED MESSAGE IS KEY

In a successful magazine ad, commercial, etc., they also don't confuse you. Coke doesn't try to sell you all their products at once. They will usually focus on one and maybe mention one other. They know that it's easy for the consumer to get confused, overwhelmed and just not buy. A lot of businesses make the mistake of advertising or telling you about all these different options and you get so confused that you DON"T BUY. You walk out, hang up or tell the eager sales person that... "I need to think about it." Or if you are hearing, "I need to talk to my spouse." You overwhelmed them, didn't get in the door, and even worst you didn't get their name, address, phone number or e-mail address!

## LESSONS LEARNED AND SHARED

- √ Really study the commercials on the main channels. The key to any business is advertising correctly! It is NOT talking to friends and family
- √ Develop your own tools. Tape yourself making

sales of your product and explaining the marketing plan or use the companies. Understand thatin order to get to the top fast you have to talk to 10,000 people a day. Go to www.chriscarley.wordpress.com and listen to the audio: How to talk to 10,000 people a day.

√ Have your retail go into a voice mail recording that says: If you are SERIOUS about wanting to lose weight, earn extra money working from home, you must leave your name number and email. I will send you a link on exactly HOW to feel great, lose weight and earn extra money in your spare time. Let this voicemail weed out the people that aren't serious and will only waste your time. Call people that have gotten results with your product or business and make an audio tape of at least 10 people. Make a product result tape and success in extra income. Get a sample of all walks of life. It should be young people, older people, single mothers, truck drivers so the people calling and listening in can identify with someone. On the product recording get people that were successful in losing weight, having more energy, sleeping better etc.

# CHAPTER 16

# SHOESTRING ADVERTISING

I often explain to those that ask for marketing and advertising advice that they don't have to spend a dime. They look at me like I am crazy. How I got started in marketing and advertising was 100% FREE. Even you can't advertise for FREE you can do it at a very low-cost. New businesses do NOT need to go into debt to find their customer.

If you are just starting out and have no money, doing these little things will also help you get the most when you do spend money to invest into advertising.

## TEST TEST TEST... THEN TEST AGAIN

Always TEST before you buy. Run a small ad before you buy a bigger ad. Most people go out and buy the biggest ad they can find. Once they find out it didn't work, they run another huge ad campaign. The problem is they find out that doesn't work as well before they can find something that does work. They are maxed out on their credit cards, and have used up all their cash reserves.

Test in a small circulation before you roll out. Remember: *The ad is successful if it pays for itself.* You will learn later in the following chapters how that one ad will also bring you upgrades, new clients and re-orders.

## THE LANGUAGE IS THE KEY

Be sure that you have the right wording for your advertising, using as many 'hot words' as possible. I don't know how many times someone has come up to me and said, "I did exactly what you told me to do and it didn't work." My reply to them is always the same: "What does your ad say?" Sometimes they don't even know!

Sometimes they spiel off a seven-line ad that doesn't have any of the advertising musts on it that cost them twice as much as a two-line ad that would have pulled better and had been tested to work!

## FREE STILL MAKES MONEY

Double the results of your advertising by using the word 'FREE' (hot word). When I first started my now million dollar business, I was so broke I couldn't afford an ad. I hand wrote my product benefits on little flyers, cards and posters. I left it anywhere and everywhere I went That's how I made my first $500. Then I discovered the power of "target marketing".

Target marketing is when you target the buyer. Imagine two teams out doing flyers. One team goes to the mall and hands out flyers. The team that uses target marketing leaves their flyers at gyms where people are already committed to looking good, losing weight or feeling better. They leave their cards on cars that are parked at a Jenny Craig or Weight Watchers meetings. They mail a flyer about their sleep product to a mailing list of people that have bought information or products on sleeping better. They leave a flyer about losing baby weight inside Parent magazines at the hospitals. This is powerful.

I used about $8.00 of my first profit and got a cheap stamp that said: "International company expanding. Pt and ft positions needed. $1,400-$4,800 per month. Call for free info book." and stamped every piece of outgoing mail on the outside of the envelope, package or folder. *I stamped extra hard on all my outgoing bills.* I used it to stamp cards and hand them out to every sales person everywhere that tried to sell me something.

Someone in real estate might concentrate on places where mortgage brokers, bank officers, or buyers live. How will they know where they live, work or how to reach them? By looking at their advertising! Everyone in the local paper who places a 'by owner' ad would be their target. Or check public records for new birth announcements, newly married, sales of homes, etc. Sometimes these people will want to or have to own a bigger house or buy their first one.

Obviously, if you have some money to invest, you can use these same principals for advertising more professionally. I have professional cards made up now and instead of looking in the paper each week or delivering a flyer door to door, I buy mailing lists and have a company mail for me. Design your advertising around your budget, not the other way around.

## SLICK ADS TO MEAN GREATER SALES

Also, if you're broke, you don't necessarily have to worry about looking professional. Just a couple of months ago I got a flyer on my doorknob. I live in a million dollar neighborhood. The flyer was typed from a home computer and I called on it! (If you don't have a computer, don't make excuses. I used the library's computer when I first started. I also used Kinko's.)

If you think this method won't work for the upscale clients you want to reach, you are missing out. Just a couple of months ago I got another flyer on my door. It was a flyer for 'peep holes'. The flyer said something about 'being safe' and 'knowing who was at the door.' It mentioned their company's name, mentioned 'references, guarantee, and free estimate.' All hot words!

I had my assistant call to get the peep hole installed. The kid came out and installed it with no problems. I told the kid that he could mention my name to my neighbors. A week later later, I noticed that three of my neighbors also had a peep hole installed. The same thing happened with lawn services, tree trimmers, pool cleaners, maid service, window cleaners, and dry cleaning businesses. I've gotten these advertisements on my door. These flyers work. My home in Florida is worth around $3 million and you can reach people like me with little or no money. *Just use the right words in your advertising.* (Stay out of anywhere where it is prohibited by law.)

## LESSONS LEARNED AND SHARED

√ No excuses! These "basic marketing" and "advertising principles" are proven. Think outside the box. I don't have a college degree, I never studied advertising, I couldn't afford to go to school or buy the books but I didn't let that stop me. Invest in yourself by taking the time to study and work on your personal growth.

√ DEVOUR the books that will change your thoughts and picture the end results you want every single day.

√ Implementing these easy strategies will allow you to cruise through that open window easily.

CHAPTER

# 17

# MANAGING THE BUSINESS YOU LOVE

Working midnight to seven in the morning and then going to three hour blueprint classes after, often I would fall asleep at work while going to the bathroom, and get woken up by pounding on the lavatory door to be written up. After too many write ups you would be fired.

My co-workers laughed at me when I asked, "Is this really all there is?" My older sister who also worked there, along with my father, grandfather, uncles, cousins sat me down and said, "Yes. This is all there is. Be happy that you have a job." I knew I was better off than millions of other people, but I also felt if I could just get some answers, some guidance, then maybe I could prove that there was a better way and I could not only help myself and my family but the millions that felt the same way I did. That's why I've written this book.

I couldn't quit, I needed money for food and rent

and I couldn't save enough to get ahead. I had no time to even try another income field after the overtime I worked and the classes I was taking to get a better job. It felt like a death sentence for me. I became sick working those hours. I became emotionally beaten up, and I finally told myself I'd had enough. I had to find a way out. The library became my mentor as I couldn't afford to buy any books and as I read the words from Zig Zigler, Og Mandino, I kept searching for answers that successful people before me had obviously found.

## NEVER LOOK BACK

As I began to discover success from the books by Wayne Dyer, Tony Robbins, Claude Bristol and my network marketing business took off, I made a promise to myself to help others even if I didn't get paid off of them. I wanted to develop a plan that would continue to maintain and multiply my success for me and my downline. So I came up with a five part maintenance program.

## PART 1: KEEP YOUR CUSTOMERS BUYING FROM YOU THE REST OF THEIR LIVES

This is obvious, but as 99% of new businesses fail, most people don't understand how to do this. Recognize your customers and clients that keep coming back or the ones that give you referrals.

Even Donald Trump does a monthly newsletter with pictures featuring members throughout, accomplishment, and events along with enticements to attend the events—generating more cash. I, along with all of the members, would clamor to see if our pictures would be in it that month.

Follow up with everyone on major holidays, birthdays, anniversaries. Use the same tools that the top billion dollar companies do! When you know one of your leaders is going through a rough time in their lives, call them. When you see someone under you doing $10,000 a month in sales, call and thank them. Recognize them by interviewing them on how they did it and put it out to everyone.

## PART 2: ALWAYS GET REFERRALS

Make sure that each customer is so happy with you that they are having all their friends, family and acquaintances buy from you. Give them an incentive to refer people to you. If you had every customer that you ever had in your business life, refer just two other people and then they referred others, your business could triple.

You don't always have to pay out money! Pay them using a product that you know could make a difference in their life. Recognition can get people to compete against each other to bring you more business.

## PART 3: GET UPGRADES

ALWAYS get the email information of every customer who has ever bought from you, or even came in to ask about your service.

ALWAYS, always, no matter if you just run into someone in the grocery line that you overhear complaining about not sleeping, low energy, hurt back-- whatever your business involves: selling mattresses, massage chairs, masseuse, or health products, or if you are or work for a doctor, take out your card (the right card) and tell them that you have the perfect thing for them to take away that problem.

Constantly take advantage of every up-to-date tool that is available. Treat your business like a million dollar business and it will respond like one! I'll say it again, because it's so important: Treat your business like it's a million dollar business. I know for a fact that Donald Trump only talks to people that have been cleared as being serious players and have the $300,000 to join.

What is better than you personally calling every single client or customer and telling them about your great new product that goes along with the one they bought? Letting the latest technology do it for you! Information CD's, DVD's, newsletters, websites, direct mailing information to people that are your target market.

How many people can you personally talk to without being exhausted? How many marriages are broken up because of 15 hour days, no vacation and no fun time? How much of your children's lives have you missed working overtime, trying to get that raise? If I am only working 4 hours a day, but getting 10 times the same results that you are working 14 hour days, seven days a week, then I am working smarter than you.

My group and I talked to over a MILLION leads a day, WHILE WE WERE SLEEPING. I first developed my retail system when I found myself repeating the same 'pitch' or information spiel 10-20 times a day, I felt like I was in the factory again! That wasn't going to work. Since I am saying the same thing over and over, why not just make a tape that would *screen* the people calling and make sure that I didn't waste any of my energy or time on someone that wasn't serious in buying.

Every single time you make a sale, give that person a sample along with information on another item or service you sell. Learn basic marketing language:

"I noticed that you were looking at the anti-ager night-cream. If you buy it today, you will get free samples of "X" or 10% off."

"I know you are here to get legal advice on your real estate, divorce, driving ticket, etc., but you also mentioned you were worried about your parents. Our office also handles senior problems, trusts, wills, estate planning... ."

## PART 4: LISTEN TO EACH CLIENT

LISTEN to each client and find out how you can help them with something emotionally. Do they tell you that their kid has asthma or trouble learning? Do they talk about how they can't sleep at night or that they are worried about their older parent's health?

If you have a health company, then include samples and information about your products that will take care of this. Make a CD or newsletter of testimonies from people that they can identify with. Let those tools do the work for you.

Whenever someone called me excited about the results that my product or business gave them, I would say, "Hold on, Sally. Is it okay if I tape this for training of my staff or others that were unsure of buying, just like you and I were?"

Stop them *before* they can tell you and record them as they tell you how great your product is. DO NOT REHEARSE THIS! If you are a Realtor, or car salesman listen to the needs of their loved ones; suggest that you can help them find the right car for their child going off to college, let them know that if they refer anyone to you, you can lower the purchase price or get them a better deal.

Do they know anyone else looking to buy a home or car? Neighbors? If they brought in the neighbor, uncle, cousin that was also thinking of buying but was going to the office across town, show them how just by getting them to come to you, they can afford to upgrade into the car with all the bells and whistles.

If they know a couple of people that are looking to sell their home, refinance, rent, give them an incentive to go out there and work for you!

Whenever someone called me and wanted my product desperately, but didn't have the money, that was the person I hired, (I didn't have to pay them, they got to earn my product!), to answers the calls that were flooding in. I made a tape of myself, live, talking to the customers that were calling for my product, so that the person could train themselves, while I was generating more business or sleeping.

The tape was with real people and their real questions (almost always the same as the calls before them) and then later I made a tape with satisfied customers whose TESTMONIES then sold anyone listening the same product, PLUS another five or six products that they had experienced results. Real people doing the work for you! In every waiting room across the world (your home office is your waiting/showroom) people are sitting with nothing to do. Put up a television with a loop of all the services you offer! If they are coming to your spa, doctor's office, showroom, use your satisfied client base to sell them on something else, more or to try that they wouldn't have normally.

## PART 5: RESIDUAL INCOME

Anyone or any business can incorporate a residual-income product that not only brings cash in when you are at your kids sports games, while you are sleeping, while you and your family are vacationing, wherever--and a consumable, residual product brings you business that grows into an avenue of income that could surpass your regular income.

I am amazed that our industry is ever under fire about income testimonies when they do not make the movie stars, sport stars and other successful 'dreamers' make disclaimers to all those tens of millions out there paying for training to make it to the big leagues when less than 1/10th of 1% will end up famous and rich. For that matter, all big companies on the stock exchange, especially ones tdhat were start-ups in their garages should have to give disclaimers that say something like: Don't think you can achieve the same success as we did because our incomes and our company's success is not the norm.

## LESSONS LEARNED AND SHARED

√ I find that those not doing well in life and business is because they are not sharing and helping others. So many times on Facebook I see a message that announces the person's success but gives no information on HOW they did it. I message that person and ask them to tell us HOW but they give me an excuse and refuse to share what is working for them or even more annoying instead of just taking a minute to message me back HOW, they call me to chat. That person just lost hundreds of thousands of dollars because if they would have shared they would have been added to my ELITE team that shares what is working for them across the world.

√ Karma works in everything. What you give out comes back to you multiplied. When you help others and come from a place where there is always enough for everyone, the right opportunities and people appear and the path becomes easy and fun.

# CHAPTER 18

# 2 CASE STUDIES OF FAILURE

When I first started in network marketing the entire company's training consisted of talking to friends and family. This is the absolute worst thing a person new to network marketing should ever do! I can't believe that so many companies still push that as a viable option, when all it does is force people to have less friends and less family.

I understood right from the start that having someone call you because they had seen your ad and were informed on your product, was 100% better than cold calling and begging others to buy something they do not know anything about. My network marketing group was doubling and tripling because I'd taken away the rejection factor. If someone saw our ad and was not interested, they would throw it away—and it did not bother us because we didn't know!

People calling us, even if they got hold of a new person who'd just joined our group who might be nervous (as I had been), knew, from our information packages, what our product does, how much it cost and since we weren't trying to oversell on a very first call, everyone calling could afford it; which made the new person pumped up!

This is an entirely different way to market, but it is also a better way to market. By focusing on customers that wanted my product I could put them through the entire success blueprint without shame or guilt. Too often I see businesses failing because they don't know how to enroll that eager customer in their success.

## CASE STUDY #1

Near my home in Arizona, my mother and I go to a nail salon that is beautiful, but chronically empty. The new owner went out of her way; offering us wine, gourmet coffee and expensive bottled water. Freshly cut flowers were beautifully spread throughout every area. Yet the owner could not understand why the place was still empty.

"It's summer, it always slows down." They answered us, when we asked where all the customers were.

Both of the nail techs had kids to feed, mortgage payments, and parents they were taking care of. They were anxious about the drop in income and talking about getting night jobs. They didn't understand that they could easily double and triple their incomes by following the principles outlined in the success blueprint.

## ADVERTISE YOURSELF

"What are you doing to advertise yourself?' I asked both of them.

They looked at me blankly.

"You should start with the client base you have now. We've been coming to you for two years and not once have you offered us something if we referred someone to you. You should have cards that you give out to every single person you work on, offering them a free pedicure if they refer five friends.

"You should have some kind of card that lets your clients know that if they come in to see you once every two weeks for a month that you'll give them one small extra treatment."

## KNOW YOUR CUSTOMER

I told them: "Develop an information card on each of your customers that tells you what they prefer and make notes on them reminding yourself of important details about your client. Their birthday, the names of their kids, whatever they've shared with you so the person bonds with you and is more likely to always ask for you and to refer their friends to. "

## THE REAL POWER OF COUPONS

I continued, "If you know the summers are bad, offer your clients a $5 off Summer Special, or first-time client special, make your own flyers at the nearest Kinko's and go next door to the Chinese restaurant and offer a special discount to the management if they'll let you leave a few flyers in the window or by the cash register.

"You can do the same for the twenty businesses that are located in this same strip mall. Talk to the owner of the salon about advertising into the homes that are in a ten-mile radius of you."

## KNOW WHERE YOU ARE MEETING YOUR CUSTOMERS

"Where have most of your clients come from? ", I asked.

"The restaurant next door." They both answered, but added: "We think."

"Where else?"

No answer.

*"You have to know.* You need to understand that anyone in sales who gets commissions or tips, works for themselves and having people come in and ask for you, specifically, will make the manager or owner wake up and see how valuable you are plus you will make more.

"I use to pay the paperboys $5 to add my flyer to the newspapers they were rolling and I had every family member and friend handing out flyers for me wherever they went. I even had nice bumper stickers that I put on my car and the cars of relatives that were helping me. I rode my bike and dropped flyers on front porches that were in a ten-mile radius of me.

"I had a 3 million dollar house on the ocean in Palm Beach Florida and I got a flyer on my doorstep advertising 'peep-holes'. You know so you can look out and see who is there? That flyer cost him almost nothing and he told me it was his best income producer. I also got my pool cleaner that way and when my landscaping guys didn't give me good service, I found my new lawn takers that way too. There are thousands of houses near here that don't know there is a beautiful nail salon right by them. You have to let them know you're here and that you offer all these different ways for them to earn a pedicure or manicure, plus advertise that your salon gives out free wine, gourmet coffee and snacks. I don't know of any other salon I've ever gone to do that!"

## HANDLING THE PHONE

The phone rang and my nail tech had to stop my pedicure and answer. She gave the person calling the prices for the treatment they were asking about and then hung up without getting an appointment. The second call, the other girl answered and the same thing happened.

"What do you do to get the person to make an appointment?" She asked, frustrated.

"The first thing you want to do is tell the person your name. You want to start a relationship. After you answer their questions you tell them that you are offering a special $5 discount if they want to book right now and you tell them about your referral program and incentive card you will give them once they come in. Then you say, "I have an opening today at—and tomorrow at—which time is best for you?"

"If they still say, I'll call you back' you say: 'Great! I'm looking forward to meeting you. Our salon is rated A, and we have twenty beautiful stations, with each chair giving you a deep massage during your treatment. We've just remodeled and offer free iced coffee and drinks."

## THE POWER OF FOLLOW UP

"Cookies!" My mom chimed in. "When I first came here they gave out free, hot chocolate cookies. I told all my friends about it and they all came in and brought their friends. We drive 20 minutes even though other salons are nearer.

"But I felt kind of bad when they all came in and you never said, 'thank you' or even mentioned that they had come in and asked for you."

Again, they both nodded.

"Don't feel bad that you've haven't done this in the past. There are a lot of businesses out there that don't follow up. Advertising works, but follow ups keep them coming back, and bringing their friends. You should know when their birthdays are and call or send a post card to them with a special 'deal' for it; or if you haven't' heard from a regular for a while mail out a 'We miss you' card with incentives and an expiration date."

## WRAP UP

My mom and I left the salon that day hoping that they would take our advice. So many service businesses find themselves struggling unnecessarily, because they forget one thing... service. As our economy matures everything has become a commodity. The actual product itself can be found on every corner of every street in every town. If you cannot differentiate yourself with world-class service, what do you really have?

## CASE STUDY #2

What I did and what you are going to do is copy the most successful businesses that you can think of. Why would we ever think that we would know more? Microsoft, Dell, McDonald's, Sprint, Sony, Nordstrom's, grocery stores chains, retail stores, *any successful company* uses the same basic blueprint to start. Why not just use the blueprint they all use?

People lose money because they go off on their

own instead of copying what has already been proven to work. They get excited about letting everyone know that they have the best product around and blow most of their money on advertisements that don't work. They go into debt, then quit their life's dream of owning their own business within the first three months, because they are broke!

## THE EMAIL

The biggest mistake I see when talking to a new person is that they think they will improve upon whatever you give them that has already worked. It's crazy.

As of this writing one of my really good golf girlfriends placed a $1,200 ad and lost all of her money. Like all the other times, of those who did this before her, she blamed me! Ignore her grammar, (English is her second language) and read her exact e-mail:

***

*Hi Chris,*

*I know you are busy, but I need at least once help, not only by email. I do not understand Leads , how this is working and also Media Share , to buy .I have sent flyers , cards, newspaper ads sent e-mails and talk , and talk to people. gave samples and have sent DVD's no response . Bought 7 Kits and products for 4000.00 $ and only sold to a friend 80. $ and signed in one person .*

*A top person and also from big check told me , I can't do it myself somebody has to show me, they all - supervisor I spoke - got it shown from their mentor .*

*I know you are not interested on me , but please*

*help as I have sold things to pay the products and I am leaving in 10 days and it is sitting under my bed until*

*Nov. Every day I spend 4 to 5 hours on H__________ and cost of $4500.00 !!*

*You did not give me one answer of my questions.*

*I feel so alone , please give me at least somebody to help , if you don't want to do it.!! Show in person as the other mentor do. On the iOffice ,I finally got it ,thanks to Naurene , but I can't find the word Task Manager " to log in the Success Workbook*

*I also signed in under you in the Touchfon since a month , never get any massage, only pay for it . In Anaheim I didn't see Debbie ,She could find me thru the Australian girls , last night I went out with them and I met nice people the 1st day and as they saw how Lonely I was , they asked me to come with them and their Mentor . Once I understand it is easy .*

***

## THIS IS WHY I WROTE THE BOOK

This is the very letter I wrote this book for. For all those out there that are confused and losing money. Be sure to take note here, she wrote this to me after I gave her everything I know, plus sent her to a three-day workshop that told her to not reinvent something that is working. Make your money and when you've got so much that it wouldn't hurt you to try something else, then go out and test your ideas.

The very important lesson here? You have to follow exactly what is working. The very first rule is: Never change an ad that is working before you test that change.

## TRUST ME I KNOW WHAT I'M TALKING ABOUT

I told her over ten times and even in writing, "Do not place an ad until I check it and make sure it is right." What do you think her response was when I e-mailed her that? It was the same response I have gotten and the people that are successful have gotten throughout the ages.

**"I DID IT EXACTLY LIKE YOU SAID!" THEY ARE SHOUTING AT YOU, BLAMING YOU.**

What do you say? "Please fax, e-mail me the ad you placed." They will argue, scream, tell you it is a waste of time and just calmly repeat yourself. After you get their fax calmly say to them, "Please get the materials out that I gave you. Go to and read me what that ad says."

There will be a pause and then you will probably here, "So, I changed it a little. You think you know everything! It is still the same ad."

No, it isn't. It may be just three words short, but it is the three words that have to be in any ad that works! "*Money-back guarantee*"?

Note here: If you are not selling something that you don't believe is the greatest thing in the world, then you are in the wrong business and you need to find something that you believe in and love. Couple that with two more words, "FREE SAMPLE!", and your ad becomes all the more powerful.

Use the age old blueprints for marketing. They are there for a reason. They give you a competitive advantage over those that ignore them.

## LESSONS LEARNED AND SHARED

√ Leaders pay attention to details. So often people trying to become leaders think that everyone is on track and by the time they find out that 10 levels deep that person isn't getting the right message it is too late and they lose good people.

√ Requiring stats each month from people will tell you when someone is off track and you can help them immediately. If you see they have talked to 10 leads and made no sales call them and find out what they are doing differently than everyone else who are making 8 out of 10 sales.

√ Sadly I have called and found out the upline who I had helped reach $10,000 a month wasn't following through with the person so I worked with that individual and that's why my check grew so fast and big. If you want explosive growth you go beneath people and work with those needing you.

√ I also found that sometimes my great leaders didn't hear me correctly even though I've told them the same things over and over. I had to create a manual with exact steps and master copies of ads that worked. Whatever business you are in, you have to have audio, video and written training because in order to learn, some people 'hear', some are visual and some need to read. Create tools in this manner that work for you so you aren't repeating yourself, so your message doesn't get watered down and constantly reinforce the things that are working by interviewing people who are growing.

√ As you start to earn a check, reinvest in your downline that are listening and following through.

Don't offer promotions of vacations or dinners, give promtions that are going to cause that person to grow instantly. Advertising that works.

# CHALLENGE

# 2

# Do each essential step

What happens if you are building a home and you don't follow the blueprint? What if you decide to leave out the foundation? These questions are basic yet some people just starting their own business leave out essential steps, intentionally or unintentionally. Then they wonder why other people in the same industry are doing better than they are. These same people find themselves going into debt just to play catch up, getting themselves no further ahead.

If you just get one thing from my book, let it be that you cannot miss the basic essentials of marketing and advertising. I have written this to reiterate how important this is. After teaching a two day seminar I reached back to some of my students after a two month time frame. Now, I know for a fact that these group of earnest and eager students understood what to do and how to implement all the marketing and advertising strategies that I had drilled into them during the two days. I asked questions, they answered back verbatim. I brought up points, they nodded their heads in agreement. Once the seminar was all over they all made the pledge to follow my example.

So imagine my horror when just two months later I talked to them. I asked them to get on our live communication system and tell the nine to fifteen thousand people listening what they got out of the 2-day training.

Some of the summation I received on my training system was, "It's not what you do, it's that you do a lot of it and you talk to more people." My mouth dropped open. I listened to the next person. "It doesn't matter if you don't know what to say, just reach more people." I instantly saw huge rejection and burnout for this person. The next guy said, "I learned that whoever has the most advertising out wins." I almost fell out of my chair. They had only understood a tenth of what I taught! It does matter what you say. Can you imagine if you are a car salesman and walk up to people and say, "Your car looks like crap. You need to buy a new one from me". Or your ad said that? You could put a million dollars into that ad and not have it pull as well as, "Test drive your dream car for free. Free estimate on your current trade-in." You do have to have the essential 'buzz words' in your ads.

The most bothersome point I had personally missed in trying to teach these new business owners, was something that I had taught but not done myself! I know from all statistics that we are only usually able to absorb 10% of new information when we are first learning. I also knew that, fundamentally, most people are either auditory, visual, or need to read in order to absorb. That would mean give a training tape, book to read and video/DVD to watch.

I love the fact that our technology allows us to answer someone back immediately. I realized that if these people were confused after being with me, a huge majority of not only new people but hundreds of people that were still struggling in my down line were also confused. I also knew from experience that no matter how loud I speak when I try to get something essential across, if I am speaking in the wrong language, they wouldn't be able to understand me. In essence, this was the message I left:

"Be very careful about just missing one step. Be especially careful about not teaching your new sales force each of the steps.

"Most all of you understand how important it is to advertise your new business. You have to understand that it is important what you say. It is important *how and where* you advertise also.

"Let's say you are selling multi-million dollar homes, country club memberships, any top-of-the-line car or service. Would you likely have a booth at the local flea market, take a full page ad out in the un-employed newsletter, weekly free paper, etc.,?
"Would you buy a mailing list of families that earn under $20,000 a year or a list of people that needed help with their debt?

"Would you take out a full page ad in a Country-Western magazine if you owned a store that sold heavy metal CD's?

"If you are selling lawn mowers, wouldn't it make more sense to direct mail to homeowners instead of condo owners or people who live in apartment communities? If you have a baby store, wouldn't you want to advertise in 'Parent Magazine' instead of

"Single's magazines? Or if you are in real estate, wouldn't it be smarter to mail to people whose listing was expiring or maybe couples that have just got married?" I took a deep breath and really annunciated, "Don't forget what you say does matter!" I went on to give them my *personal testimony*. "When I first answered an ad that was direct mailed to me on a health/weight loss product the guy that placed the ad said to me, 'How fat are you?' I was so stunned; I just hung up on him. I know I said this before but that guy lost millions of dollars because if he had answered the phone right he would have signed me.

"Listen to your training tapes. Read the books that have been out there for years that are still top sellers because they are so valuable.

"And always, always remember, test an ad first. The cheapest most inexpensive way you can do it. Put flyers in the neighborhood first, leaving your card in all the places where you know your best customer base is, maybe putting a step-like poster next to an advertising bench before you buy the bench ad—if that is legal in your area. If whatever you did, paid for itself, keep it going and make it bigger. If that works, expand the area and get control of it. Be dominant in that area. OWN YOUR OWN BACKYARD! Every one of my top producers, but one, came within a 30 mile radius of me in Auburn, WA. The one that didn't came from Wisconsin and he developed a line where all five of his top earners came within the same mile radius getting him a monthly check of over $60,000 once he implemented my materials. Ask for discounts if you run more than one week or use more than one paper. Follow up on every single lead and get referrals, upgrades, go through *every single essential step!*"

I really emphasized that last sentence and then

pushed the ‘send’ key and boom it went out to thousands of people. Now I am pushing my send key and giving it to you. Do all of the steps, before you cry failure. Only then do you know if you have a winning system on your hands or not.

# *Hope*

*"For things to change, I have to change.*

*For things to get better, I have to get better. "*

*~Jim Rohn, author My Philosophy for Successful Living*

# CHAPTER 19

# 40,000 PEOPLE

When I decided to write this book I realized that my transition from factory worker to network marketer didn't happen overnight. In fact, in the beginning I was reluctant. I didn't want to be scammed or taken advantage of. Once I got going though, it still wasn't all roses. There was a constant battle with my outer reality and the inner reality I was working to reshape.

## THE DIFFICULTY OF EVOLVING

"Write this down: "For things to change, I have to change. For things to get better, I have to get better. My spouse doesn't need to change, nor my family, job or my circumstance need to change. For things to change for me, I have to change....."

Jim Rohn gave these words to all of us attending his speech, instructing us all to put these words up somewhere we could see it and read it out loud 3 times a day for 90 days, consecutively. He cautioned us that only 1 in 40,000 would follow through—"Some of you will follow through for 30 days, then miss a day or forget to do it three times a day, and have to start over again." He smiled and waved his arm around the whole stadium.

"Some of you will make it to 60 days." Pausing dramatically, challenging each one of us, his smile got even bigger.

"Some of you will make it *almost* to 90 days...." His voice grew pained as he drew out, *almost.*

"ONE." He emphasized strongly, paused and continued, "ONE of you will make it all 120 days and *that* person will be up here on stage with me, earning millions." Forty thousand people started clapping, but he motioned with his hands to stop and we waited, sitting forward, anxious for his next instruction.

"Tape up your goals." he continued, "Somewhere in your home where you will see it the most and read it out loud 3 times a day for 120 days, *consecutively.*"

"Your first step in reaching success is to know what you want and to remind your subconscious everyday what it is. Do NOT worry about the HOW. WRITE DOWN WHAT IT IS YOU WANT!"

My teeth began to chatter as electricity flew through me. His words activated knowledge hidden in my DNA. High school teachers had taught us that the earth generates its own magnetic field, but they never went into, how. How did all the planets know to line up in just the exact right positonsconditions? What force, what Intelligence keeps the universe in perfect order? Religions from around the world call it different names but it is still the same—there is a guiding intelligence we are all able to tap into.

"I want to knooooow" he shouted into his microphone, "Who's it going to be?!" Forty-thousand people from 47 different countries exploded out of their chairs, raising their hands, shouting "Me, it's going to be me!"

Still hunched over my notebook, a stack of sticky-notes in front of me, writing my goals down on each small square clearly and furiously, I didn't even look up, didn't realize I was the only one in the stadium still seated.

*If one sticky note put up for that amount of time would make me a millionaire, how much would hundreds of little notes stuck up everywhere* make me?

√ $10,000/month checks

√ Safari in Africa

√ Porsche

√ Beach House in California *on the water*

√ Travel the world helping others

√ Have great Friends

√ Cruise the world

√ Help family buy homes

√ Charity

## WHAT WE ALL KNOW

Jim Rohn reinforced what we all know. Our thoughts, what we focus on, what we dream about, talk about, opens us to ideas that lead us to opportunities, making us understand how powerful and intricate the human body and mind is. Jim was reigniting something inside me and I felt *hope.* A dangerous feeling if you haven't a plan, but invigorating, exciting if you've got a map showing you a way to reach your goals.

## CHAPTER

# 20

# MY LEARNING CURVE

As I write this, I am still shaking my head at what transpired after I finally learned the simple rules of marketing. The same set of rules that thousands of successful people and companies had been using for hundreds of years. I made it. I had become successful, made millions in just a few years. I had done well, in spite of all of my friends and family telling me that I was a dreamer. Regardless, of them saying that I would go into debt. Even though they said that starting my own business, working from home, was impossible or limited.

Don't get me wrong, I was scared when I finally made the decision to try yet another business. Like so many others, I had tried different avenues, been taken advantage of, promised success if I invested. I lost not only my money, but my confidence. Looking at the mansions and large homes in every single city in the world—some of these homes were people's second and third homes-- I was angry at myself that I couldn't figure out what so many other people were doing to be successful. What was wrong with me that I couldn't even earn enough for one home? This was both my shame, frustration and motivation.

## SHARING THE GOSPEL OF ABUNDANCE

Traveling the world, teaching these principals, I have helped thousands; *tens of thousands* of people from all over the world, *in over 70 countries!* These men and women have come from every conceivable background you can imagine. Each person with their own special set of circumstances. All of them with one goal in mind, to build a business *within a business* that earns a residual income.

I have known brilliant doctors with strong practices who weren't able to take off an afternoon to attend their child's big game or important event. These same people are now applying the marketing principles in this book, not to just make more money, but to make more time. While they are enjoying their families and attending these important functions, their income doesn't stop. This is significant no matter who you are. The true abundance is the ability to regain your time.

## TAKING AWAY YOUR EXCUSES

Evolution isn't an easy road in the beginning. A myriad of excuses get in the way of making the transition from the old you, to the new you. I hope that I will be able to take away every excuse you have ever had.

Let me list a few of the excuses I have heard and all the reasons *I* used... .

*"I don't have enough time to do what you did."*

*"It won't work for me because I have to work full time, take care of my children, my parents and don't have a dime to invest."*

*"I have to work full time, go to school, and make time for my wife, husband, girlfriend, kids... .."*

*"My children take all my time. I can't sacrifice what they need... .."*

*"I don't know anyone who would buy from me".*

*"I have no family, no spouse or friends to support me in my dreams".*

*"I'm dyslexic and am not smart enough to keep books and records".*

*"I don't own a car",*

*"I don't feel good and I can't get out of bed... "*

*"I'm Blind, Deaf, have only one limb... .."* (Actually you won't hear these excuses because the people I helped who had any of these issues never made excuses!)

*"That may have worked back then, but things are different right now."*

This is my favorite!

The approach that's been outlined in this book has always worked and *will always continue to work.* The ideas (or principles) are not a fad or scam. Once you learn them you can incorporate them into every part of your lives. Using them I helped a single mother of three who was living out of her car, with no phone, earn $2,000 in eight days. She handed out handwritten fliers, just like I did, using the phone booth near the car she was living in. It is not the circumstances that hold anyone back, it is how you define yourself by those circumstances that makes all the difference.

All the above excuses are actual reasons I have heard and continue to hear even today. They are also some of the ones I used! This very day I will hear that excuse from people who I have helped build incredible incomes,but are now struggling as their business fails.*because* They stopped what was working and got side tracked buying someone else's materials that weren't tested!

## STAY THE COURSE

It is so easy to let the latest, greatest 'trainer,' with the bright *new* tools they want to sell you, shift you from what is working. Unfortunately, as I demonstrated through my own experiences, many of these trainers don't give you the full picture on how they truly achieved their success. So when you make an attempt to use their shiny new tool you feel like you are the one to blame, never once looking to see that the tool itself was flawed.

After helping build thousands of people who were desperate and broke after following the wrong plan for years, I was stunned when they reached the top and decided they would rewrite the materials that got them there. I would standby, helpless, as I watched groups consisting of thousands of successful people stop using what was working and switch to something untested. In those instances I have never been more frustrated and sad.

That is why I always say 'stay the course'. If you have something new, TEST it along side what worked before. Don't abandon one for the other, because it rarely turns out in your favor.

CHAPTER

# 21

# KNOWLEDGE IS POWERFUL

In just a few years of going to the "Temple" *(library)* that stored the "Answers" *(marketing success after success)*, I went from being a $10.50 an hour, fired, airplane factory worker to earning over a million dollars. All of this accomplished byincorporating marketing materials that did all the work for my team and I.

Today, I have a lifestyle that has allowed me to golf and hang out with Donald Trump and get to know him as a friend. I have met people like Barbara Walters, Katie Couric, former President Bill Clinton, and former President Gerald Ford, along with so many more. Movie stars have filmed or been photographed in my Malibu home; George Clooney, Cameron Diaz, Lucy Liu, Drew Barrymore, and Bruce Willis, to name a few.

I shake my head as I write this, remembering how desperate and physically ill my factory job left me. Working midnight to 7 in the morning, I cried every night on my way to work. At the time I didn't know what the universe had in store for me, and I kept 'seeing' the future I wanted and didn't give up. I still read my motivational books even though I was ridiculed. I still stood up for myself, when no one else would, and I still persevered when everyone and everything seemed to be against me.

## WHO ARE YOU TRUSTING WITH YOUR DREAMS AND FUTURE?

When I would get a call or message from someone who just lost their life savings or the kid's college fund, lamenting: "I did what my mentor told me to do and it didn't work!" I would be sick. Don't let this happen to you.

Who are you listening to? *Anyone* who wants to give you advice, ask them, "LET ME SEE YOUR CHECK."

When dealing with anyone trying to get you into a business deal, franchise, or sell you an ad, always ask to see their results. It is not a perfect method, but it's a method that quickly weeds out the pretenders who want to make a fast buck off of you. No system is perfect and with my current success I have not been immune. Even with my due diligence efforts and expanded circle of influence I still find that it's difficult to determine what the truth really is.

## WHAT IS GURU ADVICE REALLY WORTH?

Whether it's sales advice, money managers, stockbrokers, network marketing Gurus, or so-called investment seminar experts, advice and training are everywhere. There is so much noise, now so more than ever, it is difficult to really know who to trust.

After working so hard to earn it, I watched my million-dollar portfolio in the stock market dive on CNN, in real time. I know marketing. I know advertising. I know sales. So as I moved up in the world I made the assumption that the financial analysts also knew about their industry. I was more furious with the analysts giving current advice on what to do, than I was about the market. They were the ones I followed in the first place!

Why didn't they show me *their* portfolios? Why didn't they tell me how much they were up or down for the year?

Then I was furious with myself. I didn't follow my own advice, and I had lost *hundreds of thousands* of dollars. WHY did I not *demand* to see how much money they had made *before* I followed their advice? Why would I listen to anyone or follow their plan without asking to see their track record? How many times was I going to invest my time, money and energy without first asking to see what it had done for them? Why was I listening to anyone if they weren't successful?When it came to network marketing I had only gone to the most successful to learn from. Why wasn't I doing the same thing in my other endeavors?

Would I have made the same decision, spent my time learning and listening to them, have my future and families' future on the line if I had found out that my mentor or teacher or advisor hadn't had success in that field? I had just assumed since they were on television, or had a book published, or were teaching a seminar, they had achieved success in that field. I found out that a lot of Real Estate 'how-to' seminar teachers/investors, some marketing seminar professionals, hadn't made any money or had actually lost money in the last ten years in that field. I found out that the only real money or success they had achieved was selling to people like me their books, tapes and videos.

This was a frustrating lesson to learn, yet it applies in all walks of life. You cannot take advice about network marketing from someone who has never been really successful in a network marketing business, nor can you trust anyone who simply markets and promotes how to be a great network marketer without finding out exactly how they did it. Insist on knowing the truth.

## THE RELATIONSHIP EXPERT

When you are first getting into a business, career position, even a relationship and are seeking guidance, check out whoever it is you are following. What are their results? I was confronted with the unreliable 'guru' phenomena once again when I bought a relationship teacher's books and tapes from an infomercial. Years later I found myself with her, backstage in 'the green room'. For those not familiar, a green room is a T.V. show's waiting room for the guests to sit in until they are called on stage.

I tried to make small talk with her, but for whatever reason she was not receptive to me. So I resigned myself to just listen to her talk to one of the other guests. I overheard her talking about her first marriage. Then she was talking about her second husband. She then mentioned what her third husband was like. She had been married a total of five times!

No wonder my marriage was falling apart. I was studying the wrong plan and obviously so was she!

## NO ONE IS INFALLIBLE

I bring up these instances, because I am not perfect.

I have been mislead by well meaning and not so well meaning people throughout my life, but never once did I stop looking for the answer I wanted and deserved. I don't consider myself a guru and want to move as far away as I can from cultivating that type of image. No matter what, I am still that hardworking factory girl who took an opportunity by the horns. That makes me understand where you are. It gives me the ability to help you pull yourself up and at the end of the day I have checks to prove it. My advice throughout these chapters is meant to do one thing and one thing only: empower you to be who you are meant to be. You don't need a guru for that, you need a friend. Hopefully, that friend can be me.

# CHAPTER

# 22

# WHEN WILL I BE SUCCESSFUL?

I turned my life around and became a millionaire in just three years. If someone had told me that they had a plan that would show me how to be a millionaire in 36 months I would have laughed at them. Yet it happened.

Without a doubt there was a confluence of events in my life at that time. I cannot promise you that you will be a millionaire or give you any type of guarantee on how much you will possibly make following my system. What I can do is ask you, "What does the alternative look like if you don't try?" I knew my alternative was to remain depressed, stay defeated, and hope I could find another menial miserable job, if I was lucky. I decided I didn't want that, so I evolved. This book is your chance to do the same.

## HOW LONG UNTIL THINGS CHANGE?

When I started out I learned very quickly that when a person is trying to sell you on following them, find out how long it took for them to get their success and what they did before that endeavor.

My first few months of trying to get my sales off the ground, I was listening to a couple who were teaching that their sales went to over $100,000 a month just the 2nd month in the business. For three grueling weeks I did EXACTLY what they told me to do.

It wasn't working. In fact, I was going backward and was burning out. I started to ask them questions. It wasn't easy to get near them either. They avoided Q&A's and any individual questions. I had to trap the wife in the bathroom! I found out that they had come from another sales company and brought over all their sales reps with them! I found out that they had been in this business over ten years but didn't count the first nine years because their first real month of 'really working' had just started. I also found out that the company I was involved with had let them teach this to thousands of other new people before me.

I actually went home and cried. I wanted to quit.

The same thing happened again, when I listened to another couple give their income testimony. They kept repeating, "All we did was talk to people." What they failed to mention was that they were entering new countries illegally, and that no one else had access to these countries. They also failed to mention that they had uprooted themselves and lived in Mexico City for years.

Here I was trying to copy them and they weren't telling me what they were really doing.

## SPECIALIZED TRAINING, NOT SO SPECIAL

One time I had paid for specialized training and flew

all the way to Hawaii to learn the secrets of a successful networker from Japan. I sat in the front row and after four hours of hearing nothing on how to improve my business, I finally just stood up and asked, *begged,* "You've been telling us for an hour now that you had so many new clients and customers that your business started booming. How did you get those customers?"

He was evasive; he didn't want to tell me. I refused to sit down. In front of about 200 top people I rephrased my questions. "You said that three nights a week you packed a room full of new customers. How EXACTLY did you pack the room?" He started to sweat. He answered, "It's easy to get customers; that's not what I am teaching."

He started showing us pictures of his great office, his Rolls Royce, and his checks. I stood again. "In your area, (Japan) you are not allowed to run any advertising. How did you pack a room? How can I learn to pack a room?"

What I really wanted to say was, "You have no right to get up onstage and teach if you aren't going to teach us how to duplicate you." The fact was, he didn't want to teach me. I would be his competition someday and he didn't want to help me.

After he was off the stage I didn't stop. By that time I had taught a lot on stage myself and had helped hundreds of people improve their sales. One of his direct associates who worked with him came up to me. He was one of the people I trained when I had gone to Japan. At that time I taught them everything I knew. I had given them exact ads, newsletters, and shared with them our sales tools for them to copy.

He may have felt guilty that his upline wouldn't share and give back because he decided to tell me the speaker's secret. It was a brilliant marketing strategy.

Japan was a very hot market and due to the speaker running illegal ads making unrealistic income testimonies, the government would no longer let any advertising into any newspapers. The top Japanese salespeople were really hurting because of this. Yet he had found a loophole. He ran ads in all the major newspapers that said, "Free English accent lessons."

He didn't speak Japanese, but his wife did. In teaching them English slang and pronunciation, he told them about his product and business opportunity.I was so naïve when I first started and you can learn from my naivety and not repeat my mistakes.

## RED HERRINGS AND MISSING RECIPE INGREDIENTS

This kind of behavior is notorious in the sales industry. A lot of speakers have huge egos and are up there to only promote themselves. You can still learn from them, though. Keep asking questions.

The only thing that saved me was concentrating on the fact that with all this deceit, this guy from Japan was making over 2 million dollars a year. I thought, let's see what I can do without using any deceit. This was a very important lesson, one I was to keep repeating. When something not quite positive happens to you, and it will, learn from it, and learn not to ever do it.

# CHAPTER 23

# THE WRONG PLAN

*"You were so real! You talked from your heart and you said it like it is. Half the words you said weren't even correct and sometimes I didn't even understand you, but I could hardly put my notebook down and I have never had such exact instructions given to me!*

*"Just the training you gave us on 'Free Samples' propelled my business further than anything else I had ever learned from any book or seminar that I have paid thousands of dollars for."*

More than one already successful CEO had waited in line just to come up and shake my hand and tell me, *"After watching the first five minutes of your DVD training, I told my wife, 'she is awful, she is all over the place and I can't even follow what she is saying,'*

*"Then with my wife eyeing me I couldn't stop myself from sitting down, closer to the TV. What you were saying really caught my attention and I couldn't stop listening. I*

*kept asking my wife, 'How much is she earning a month?' When for the third time she told me, 'Over $10,000 a month' I grabbed some paper and started making notes! You had already showed me how to place an ad that really worked, that one tip could have stopped my last venture from draining our life savings! As I watched you talking from your heart, I started to laugh and nod my head in agreement, finally really getting it and I just knew that I was going to get rich!"*

## WHAT I HAVE TO SHARE

I know what he was really thinking. If that 'non-educated hick' farm girl can make that much money, then with my college and Masters degree, plus years of experience, I am going to make even more than her!

Great! That is exactly what should happen! This particular gentleman reached his goal in just three years. The very first time I met him he came right up to me and said, "If you think you can ever get me making more money than I do now and quit my job of over 20 years with Boeing Aerospace, you really are crazy.

"I'm going to help my wife part time, but I don't believe you even make this much."

Who could blame him? I was still in my 30's and even though I held a copied check of over $20,000 for that month and also had the previous checks from EACH month for the last several months laid out before me showing each check increasing every single month, I still had trouble believing it!

I wonder what would have happened to both of us if we were to know then that my check would keep growing every single month for the next several years to way past $100,000 a month!

## THE WRONG 30 YEAR PLAN

As I got to know him better, I understood why he was so afraid that I would help him reach his goals. It was the same reason why so many of us don't bother to even look into something like this. If what I was saying was true, that meant that he, now in his fifties at that time, had been following the wrong plan for over thirty years! No one wants to admit that.

This is the really sad part for many of us. How can we let go of the idea that we've spent hundreds of thousands of dollars on a degree and 30 years of our lives in a job that we really didn't even like? How can we let go of an investment (our job) that we have invested five if not seven days a week into. Not including all of the special training, continuing education classes, travel, time away from our families, missing our children growing up.

In addition to all of that, my friend had been spending two hours every morning and two hours every evening, without getting paid, driving to and back from his life's career. How could he possibly admit that all those years following that plan had been wasted? He didn't have to and neither do you!

Every single minute, every single second, of all those years, we get to take them with us! After just the first week of incorporating what I taught him into his normal work day, he tested and experienced results right away. Quickly drawing upon all those years, all those hours, and all those overtime weekends, he and his wife started to break income records right behind me!

## WHAT MADE THE DIFFERENCE

My friend later went on to India and Dubai to lead

one of the strongest financial teams in the Seattle area. So what made the difference? He followed some basic tenets when he decided to step out of his comfort zone:

1. At least try.
2. Understand that if thousands of people were making it work (especially a fired ex-Boeing worker) then he could too.
3. Realize there is nothing wrong with changing your blueprint if a new plan or machine does the work faster and easier.
4. He decided that the only waste would be staying in the old plan even longer! At that time, according to the national mortality stats of a man's life after he went to full retirement—age 65-- was just two years, horrific.

My grandpa worked for that same company and he retired at age 60 and although he didn't die at 62, he became really ill, and all those fishing trips he promised to take me on when he retired never happened, because he didn't feel well enough to go.

## JUST COPY IT!

What about your plans? Are you waiting to get married, waiting to have kids, waiting to take that big vacation until you get enough money or get that promotion? This is the wrong plan!

Learn how to reach all your goals while you are on that vacation, building that new home, riding in that new car. Instead of, "Just do it" (you've been trying, you need to know how!), then: 'JUST COPY IT!' Follow through with the marketing plan secrets detailed in this book. Secrets that are in plain sight. Copy me, who copied the big guys, and see similar if not the same results!

Getting started and showing a profit with next to nothing. Remember, I did it with as little as $8.00 for my first hand-written posters! This is my purpose for writing this book is to teach you how to succeed right from the start. I have one goal in mind for you, to put money in your pocket right away without going into debt.

CHAPTER

24

# SUCCESS AT WORK

When I first started learning, I was so disappointed that a lot of books were out there just to hype the reader up and get them to buy more tools. So many times I would take valuable time and money only to get to the end and there wasn't any meat or substance, I could incorporate into what field I was in.

Even the massive amount of training I paid for, but couldn't really afford, that advertised that the student would learn how to make millions, made me want to scream. Speaker after speaker got up and told 'their story', all the hardships they had incurred and then showed us their fancy cars, homes etc., and never taught me how to achieve the same results.

In fact, during one three-day training I attended,I actually slept in a bathtub, because I was sharing a hotel room with four other gals who were just as broke and confused as I was on, attending a 'how to' become successful training, I finally had had enough. That's when I decided to rely on marketing basics to help me.

## SUCCESS THROUGH COPYING

Whenever I would bring someone into the business I would make it as easy as possible for them. I would start by saying, "Do you love this product and want to market it? Great, you are already trained and you can start right now. Remember how I gave you a sample and some info and then you called me and ordered it after a couple of days... . That's all you have to do now to get going. It's really that easy!"

People would be skeptical and look at me as if I had two heads. It couldn't be that easy. It couldn't be that simple. Yet, it was then and it still is just that simple now.

## THE RIGHT MARKETING WORKS FOR ANY BUSINESS

I remember I met a young lady, a technician, at a spa I liked to go to. She knew my story and asked me for tips on how to promote her business and increase her sales on her eyelash products. I get questions like this all the time. Many people simply don't follow through. So I half expected the same when I went to get a facial from her the next time I went in.

Of course the first thing I noticed was the technician's lovely eye lashes. They were incredibly long and thick from the last time I saw her. I wanted to ask her right then what she had been doing, but waited to see if she had gotten all the marketing ideas I had given her correct from the last time I had been there. I had to laugh when she let me get into the robe where she had put a little card on top of it that read: Longer lashes in 2 weeks, guaranteed!

The product was retailing for $150.00, a ridiculous amount, but she had listened and told me, "I'm offering all my best clients a 30% discount if they buy today. I also have referral cards for you to hand out." The wholesale price was around $60.00, but none of the other technicians at this expensive spa were doing the things I had taught her and not only did she outsell all ten of her co-workers, even with the 30% discount, her commissions for one week were more than triple of those who had sold without any kind of incentive.

The next time I saw her, I gave her a little button she could pin onto her coat that had two eyes closed with beautiful lashes and under them said, "Ask me about my long eyelashes". She forgot one thing I had taught her, that was leaving a lot of money in commissions on the table for her. I had stressed to her how important it was to have real testimonies, especially before and after pictures.

Right there she whipped out a camera and took a picture of my 'before' lashes. When she was done with my new lashes she took another photo and two weeks later, when I stopped back in, she had them *up on her wall.*

No matter how good the company literature is, everyone wants to see 'REAL' people. All of us are tired of seeing models and if you ask ten people who look at your home-made before and after pictures and compare them to your slick promotional brochures, they will tell you they bought the product or the procedure because of the home-made advertisement. I was tremendously proud that she had asked for advice and then applied it. If the owner of the spa trained all of the staff in the same way, not only would they make more money, but the customers would be even happier.

## RIGHT BUSINESS, WRONG CARD

In my walks of life I receive thousands of business cards. Very rarely has anyone given me a business card that brings value to me, the potential customer. Something so simple, yet 95% of people are losing thousands of dollars in commission, company growth, referrals, upgrades, all because of an unnecessary mistake. In fact the majority of business cards will be thrown away, because of these mistakes!

So let me give you a few insights right away so at least the next time you get your cards printed, you won't be missing out on a bunch of $$$$.

## FROM BUSINESS CARD TO SALES CARD

Obviously you will have your name, address, phone, email address, website, fax and a brief description of what your business is, for example:

Suzy Jones Bob Jones

*Realtor Attorney*

Business cards should really be called "sales" cards. Not only should the card give information about your business, they should be made in such a way that anyone finding it, would not throw it away, but keep it—just in case they would someday use you or refer you to a friend. This is a card that gives added value to the customer.

How do you do this? I will try and hit as many different business examples as possible. Obviously some will only apply to a certain business, but I am sure you are smart enough to match it up and come up with ideas for your own business.

Your card should:

1. Make the recipient an offer.

   Example of an offer: Free test drive when presenting this card. Free Samples with this card. Free drinks when you purchase a meal. 10% off all computer packages with this card. Free market analysis of your home's worth. Free landscaping consultation. Free ½ hour consultation of legal services.

   Usually you will even see that a person has three or four cards of your competitor in their wallet, so how do you make sure they call you once they get home and remember who is who or who said what... ..

2. Give an incentive to buy from you (and not your competitor.)

   We pay *you* for referrals, (Check what is legal for your industry but remember this doesn't have to always be cash). I once got a referral of a round of golf at a very prestigious course that would have cost me at least $400.00 for referring a couple of people to my Realtor who subsequently bought a home from him.

   My favorite restaurant owner, to whom I sent numerous groups of high spending customers, will not let me pay for a meal whenever I come in. When I didn't come in for a while, because I didn't want to take advantage, they called me and sent over hundreds of dollars worth of takeout.

My masseuse gave me free massage and a very expensive package of lotions after I had sent her two customers who hired her for weekly massages.

My dive shop nearby is so incredible. Whenever I refer groups to them they are always asking me to go along when there is room, and will not let me pay.

The mortgage broker, who I have sent many people to, sent over a case of expensive wine.

Just about anyone you come into contact with, where you will be using their services and they are exceptional, you can talk to them and barter your cards and referrals when you agree to recommend them. For example: Landscapers, attorneys, hair dressers, nail techs, accountants... .

Other incentives that can be offered:

We guarantee our price. We strive for life-long relationships, % discount with contract for service. Free rental for service check- ups when you buy a Mercedes. Free acupuncture service when you join our Wellness Center.

3. List one or multiple reasons to never throw away the card, and make them ask you if they can have more cards to hand out for you.

"Bring three new clients to our studio and get one month free personal training; gym dues paid or yoga class. Two for one dinner entrees, Send five of your friends with this card and get your dinner paid for."

**ASTON MARTIN DEALERSHIP SECRETS (YOU MIGHT BE SEEING A PATTERN)**

As you have probably figured out from

reading this book, I like cars. Some of these ideas were points that came from a great salesman at an Aston Martin Dealership I visited.

The first salesman I met had a plain card and hadn't bothered to use his business card as a sales card. I walked out not buying and really not being interested in buying. Nevertheless, something kept nagging at me and I really wanted to learn more about that car.

When I went back to look at it again, another sales person gave me his card. On the card were a bunch of reasons why to buy the car from him. He offered a free rental car when my car was being serviced. He also offered a pick up service. So I bought the $175,000 DB7 from him and threw the other guys' card away. I was kind enough to tell the first salesman that he should change his business card to a sales card and the next time I saw him, he had!

You want to make every card you give out an advertisement so that if anyone found it on the ground they would want to keep it for the day when they will want or need your product.

Most cards I see, I don't even know what the person is selling! Have your cards made as if they were a small ad in the best paper, magazine or billboard and if you had all the money in the world to spend, you would have your card reflect this.

## SUCCESS DOESN'T COME CHEAPLY

Very few people are born with the innate set of tools that will make themselves successful. Success is a habit that needs to be cultivated. It begins with many small victories, some setbacks, and then more victories, so on and so forth. It's the setbacks that stall too many people. They use the setbacks to give up, to quit, and to stop innovating. Let success be a habit for you. Let everyday's small victory be a reason for celebration and the big victories will follow.

## CHALLENGE

# 3

## Be the 1 in 40,000!

Take Jim Rohn's challenge.

Write this down:

"For things to change, I have to change. For things to get better, I have to get better. My spouse doesn't need to change, nor my family, job or my circumstance. For things to change for me, I have to change....."

Put your goals somewhere you can see them and read them out loud 3 times a day for 120 days, consecutively.

Your first step in reaching success is to know what you want. The second step is to remind your subconscious everyday what it is. Do not worry about the how. Write down what you want first and the how will come to you.

# Conclusion

*"Focus. On. The. Ones. That. Deserve. It."*

*- Mark Hughes*

## YOUR JOURNEY IS JUST BEGINNING

"Gramps, I can catch anything that comes to me and I am a good hitter, but compared to all the older kids, my legs are too short and I can't run the bases as fast as them." I told Grandpa, frustration in my voice.

When gramps got excited or he had something important to say, he would grin, lick his lips and start stuttering sounding like an engine that wouldn't kick over.

"Thaaaaa, Thaaaaat, That's eeeeasy to fix... ".

He always talked slow making sure I was really paying attention.

He grabbed my two hands and pulled me close, getting ready to tell me a secret I'd be able to use the rest of my life. "If you hit the ball over the fence, you can *walk* the bases."

## WHY I WROTE THIS BOOK

I have had my successes, but I promised God a long time ago, that I would give back and help others. This is me giving back. This simple, easy book is written for the thousands of individuals I see and meet throughout my life who live paycheck to paycheck, or just above.

People's whose retirement isn't sufficient, People whose retirement is insufficient. People who toil away in jobs they dislike. Individuals who are desperate to learn how to get ahead. People who are praying for a way to change their future.

I meet these people waiting tables at restaurants where an expensive meal and bottle of great wine cost more than what they bring home in a month. I see their questioning looks as they park my car that costs more than their home.

This book is written for old and current friends who are making just above minimum wage. It's for dozens of family members working long hours to keep their families fed, employees who work for me: the young pool cleaner, the hard working gardener, the elderly man who washes and takes care of my boat and the bevy of yachts in front of my house, the breathless, overworked valets who run in 100 degree heat parking hundred thousand dollar cars at Donald Trump's private golf club; the stewardess in private planes who stoically take abuse from spoiled owners and the hundreds of worn out unemployed workers waiting in line.

I notice them all, because I was one of them for most of my life. Work weary individuals who are just slightly missing riches because they don't know the basic rules of getting ahead in life.

## YOUR JOURNEY

All you need to do is START the exercises, follow the examples, and then reach out to me and let me know how well they have worked for you. Send me emails on my website, and blog www.chriscarley.wordpress.com, like me on Facebook,

Tweet me, etc. Join my community and contribute to our entrepreneurial dialogue. Or you can do it the old fashion way and send me a letter telling me how you have used my experiences to change your life.

My greatest mentor had a conversation with me before he passed away. We were talking about my need to give back and the enormity of the company he had created from scratch. In that conversation he let me know you can't help everyone but you can "Focus on the ones that deserve it." That has stuck with me.

You have found my book. You have made it to the end. You are one of the ones that deserve it. Now go change your life.

# APPENDIX

# 1

# Transcribed Speech Chris Carley gave in Australia

[clapping]

**HOST:** Thanks everybody – good morning everybody, I'd like to welcome you down here today for incredible training, and I know some people have traveled a long way to be here today and it's very, very exciting. The first thing I'm going to say today, is Chris Carley, is one of the top success trainers in the world, she's not just company specific, she's being touted as a female Tony Robins, she's not just built her own business's she's been invited by many successful corporations around the world to help them build their sales teams and their businesses as well. Associates that worked for the likes of Oprah Winfrey, Mercedes Benz, Coca Cola and even Donald Trump have asked Chris Carley to come in and help them with their teams and their sales teams.

So the skills you're going to learn today from Chris are not just business specifics to the business you're in now, they're specific to anything you want to do in any area of your life – success secrets, personal growth, the whole gamut of success, information is coming from Chris today. So what I'd like you all to do today is be up standing and a riotous round of applause for Miss Chris Carley!

[heavy applause, cheers, dozens of fans rush stage for autographs]

Okay, how about we do this at one of the breaks! [laughter] Think and grow rich, wow – pretty soon you guys will all have my book. Okay, well we should do this during the break. Okay. Boy, I'm very, very excited to be in Australia, it was one of my dreams to be here in Australia, to go down under. I'm telling you, it means a lot to me – Steve Patterson bothered me so much for the last two years to come here, and arranged for me to be here. Today I'm going to do a course in success, okay, and I really really wanted to see children here. A child is most impressionable between the ages of 9 and 12. Where's Brad? Brad is our only – what are you, 14? We have anybody else? Emma. Congratulations because the things you're going to learn here too you're going to be able to apply in school, in sports, I'll teach you guys about girls. [laughter] How to succeed there. And you're going to be able to take this everywhere you go, some of you guys I know have different occupations, I don't care if you're a doctor or you're in real estate or cars or if you're a teacher, you still need the skills on how to sell you. And everything that you do. Same if you're competing for a sport or you're competing in anything that you can think of, in a relationship you need certain skills, and I'm going to teach you how to get those.

You're going to learn from this life seminar from each other too because we're going to bring some of you guys up, and I'm going to learn, I'm not going to be the same person after today, neither are you. We're going to make a successful course training system where maybe one word that you say, maybe one story that you tell would affect not hundreds of people, not thousands of people, but millions of people. You never know that you triggered something that changed somebody's life forever, that you shared somebody or got something. This is also why you want to utilize everybody that you have, because you could say something to the people in your employment or the people in your family or the people that are looking at you as a mentor, you can say what I' going to say over and over again and this happens to me, and all of the sudden, somebody will say the exact same thing I've been saying for five years, and somebody will say, wow did you hear what they said? And it's because for some reason they identified with that person and they didn't with me. That's why you always want to utilize, and you don't ever want to be the issue because something somebody else says can trigger one thing that can change a person's life, health, relationship with their children, you know, with their life.

I think that's why we're here. I think we're put here to help each other, um, to not live mediocre lives, and I think everybody's entitled to be, and have every single dream that they want, realized, I do not think you could have a dream if you couldn't realize it, and I'm living proof of it.

So, these things that you're going to learn today, you're going to be able to pass on to family members that you couldn't get here – that maybe laughed at you for wanting to improve your life, wanting to start your own business, wanting to make a difference in the world.

Um, and you're going to be able to pass onto them, and maybe just even again, one thing that they'll change that made their lives so different. I started doing that when I was young, when I was ten years old, and this story will fit in with not only kids but will fit in with everybody.

I was raised on a farm, my dad was a blue class worker which means in America, you know, I don't know how to say this without offending every blue class worker, it hard, he was in a machine shop and he ran a machine, we struggled from paycheck to paycheck,Boeing aerospace is one of the biggest, you know, aerospace's and manufacturers in the world and but the mentality that we were brought up with is, you work for a big company, and you're going to be safe. You work for a big company and you're going to have an income that you can always count on. Well he got laid off three or four times, I can remember going on where we had to be on some kind of a supplement program to get some of our lunches paid, I can remember lots and lots of fighting and I can also remember the fear of, I am not going to leave my destination or what I can accomplish or what I can get under somebody else. I wanted to be the one that's going to decide what's going to happen to me.

So we were raised out on a farm, I couldn't get a paper route, there wasn't a lot to do out there, I couldn't go mow lawns, and I was a kid and my father—my father when I wanted a motorcycle and I wanted a horse or anything, he said sure, I thought he was so mean back then, he said you earn half of it. I'm like what would you like me to do? I'm too little to even push a lawnmower, that just about killed me – he said why don't you focus on what you can do, so I thought and thought, there were three neighbors, I could walk over there and stuff like that, I was in sixth grade – how old was I? I can't even add. 11 or 12. I went over to one neighbor who had four children, went over to her, and knocked on her door and introduced myself, said I'd like to baby-sit. She said oh, you know, if you never need anybody, would like to earn some extra money. She said actually I need somebody every single day, but you're too young. And I've already got one of the other girls and she's going to come over and she's three years older than you.

And I was really really depressed and I went home and I was like that's it. So then I started to think though, what could I offer, because I knew this girl and I knew that she wasn't outgoing, I knew she maybe wouldn't play with them like I would, I really liked the kids – what I did was, I wrote down every single asset that I thought that I could give her more than this girl could, without putting her down. I didn't say, I'm much better at playing with children than she is, I actually saw her beating up a kid. I didn't do that. She was not the issue, okay? And this is what you're going to do with your competition. They're not the issue. What they're doing, if it's unfair or if it's mean or ugly, they aren't to the issue, you are.

Went back to her house, gave her this little sheet, and she read – she was really impressed, she said I'm really happy with this girl, so for 8 weeks I'd go up there and knock on the door and ask her if she was still happy and yes she was and then I said okay, if anything ever happens to this girl, I'm ready. She was thinking, this girl as young as she is, I could – see something in her. So Lisa got sick one day, and this is what I want you to do in your business no matter what business you're in, no matter what you're going to apply this to, and soon, so I got to baby-sit. As soon as she left, I sat the kids down and said, what does Lisa do all day with you? Because this was a big thing, this was Monday through Friday and there was a lot of money here. They said, in a chorus, she watches TV. I'm like, oh. I said does she play with you at all? No. Does she clean up the kitchen at all? No. Does she tell you stories, help you with your homework? No. Guess what I did? That day, cleaned the kitchen, folded the clothes, played with the kids, I had them all clean by the time she came home and I got that business. And she called me now, instead of her. And that's what you've got to think about, in whatever avenue that you're in, I know couples will do this, when you're pursuing and wanting somebody to go out with you, you just think of – if you really really want it, then you look at what's happening there and you figure out a way you can give them better service and you can do more follow-up and you can become more...

Now how would a kid that's 10-12 years old know to do this? I was reading books at that age, my favorite book obviously when I was a lot younger was the little train that could, and I just always always and I do to this day, believe that I don't care what's going on with you, you can learn to beat every odd that there is and to be more and to realize every single thing that you want. How do I know this? One, I did it, and two, thousands and thousands of people are doing it. So the difference between you and them, is that you're not doing something that they're doing. Okay? Um, we have a communication system, where I have trained over and over again, and scientists have proven, this isn't something I'm just throwing out there and talking out of my you know what – scientists have proven, you'll see people interviewed – Tiger Woods in golf, you'll see Lee Iacoca, you'll see that Harry Potter kid that's playing that – that actor. 90 % is your mind.

So what are you doing – I mean I did the figures really quick, if 90 % of my success is based on my mind, then I better put 90 % of energy into what, my mind. Okay. Now I've trained over and over and over again that you have got to feed your brain, and your soul and your heart and you've got to learn and do exactly what you know, somebody who's earning, I don't even know what I earn, $200,000 a month, whether I work or not, is doing. Okay, and I have told you guys, you wake up in the morning, the first thing you do is, you need to read. You know Australia better than I do, you might know some place else better than I do, these people, first of all, you in Australia, we have the world that you can work with, maybe we might not have our materials in a certain country or in a certain place, but sooner or later we will – I will. So you can still put it out and plant some seeds, and you've got to think, I want to know and understand this American business because I want Americans, and I want my children to go over and you know, and have a party with Chris and go to Donald Trumps and meet and see this lifestyle, I want my children to see that. So I've got to learn, and you've got to treat your people that are listening to you the same way. They, you know, so many of you guys, there's a big huge world and you're – you don't understand that you have the right to experience that. Yes you want to stay in your own back yard, you want to get that, but you also want to be open, so you've got to be very very careful, so what I would do anyway is I didn't pass it, I called up the person and said look, I don't understand your thoughts behind this, could you explain it to me, and the explanation was horrifying, so I'm still sitting there, and I said okay, would you mind telling me how long you've tested this that you just told everybody.

I just started it. That really is something that you never want to do. Sometimes I think I have the most brilliant ideas in the world and I don't put them out there until we've tested them. I had a brilliant idea, you've got all these homeless people in the street with a sign begging for money, right, well, instead of holding that sign, why don't they hold my sign? It doesn't cost me anything. So I didn't put it out to the group and I tested it, well that's not a good look, to have somebody – got the shakes from last night, and I drove by and saw that and I thought my goodness, not a good idea. Luckily I didn't put that out, and also when you put out stuff that you haven't tested, especially when you put it out, when you're running a team of sales forces or even your employees or whatever, and you put something out that you didn't test, and you keep doing that and getting everybody all confused – one, they're going to get where they don't trust you any longer, and two they're going to really get frustrated. So you don't put something out until you test it, but you also don't be dumb enough not to – when you see somebody doing a huge, and breaking all records, that you don't check out what they're doing.

You know, somebody said to me, all training is the same. The advertising that you do, really it's all the same, I said no it's not, there was a point of time where my training was bad, and my manuals were bad and it wasn't the best thing out there, so you want to always know and be open enough and smart enough, to think that I can always always improve, if there's a better website out there than mine, I need to know about it and I need to study it.

If somebody's doing more in my area than I am, I need to know about it, I need to go to it, you know, I have this friend who owned a restaurant, incredible food but there were no people coming in. you know, I get paid to go into peoples' business, and I just love it because it helps me, helps them, and the same principles are going around and around and around. The people were negative, the people weren't reading, the people had no motivational things but the number one thing that I see everywhere in almost any business, and what the top people including Bill Gates, Donald Trump, all those people and all those guys know is that there's three reasons why people do the things they do, so if you want your spouse or your child, or your girlfriend or boyfriend or whoever, to do things, you've got to know these three things. You want your buddies to do something, I'm not talking about manipulation here, the three things are love, money and recognition. Now what do you guys think is the number one out of those three?

See I always thought it was money and then I thought it was love and then I started to think about why I did what I did, breaking all sales records, studying so hard, turning off the TV, not going out and it was because I wanted to get close and – to the people at the top, I wanted to get to know them and nowhere else that I've ever worked for had they ever really recognized me, and I wanted my recognition, so you want to recognize people, okay, and you want to encourage good habits, you know, I'm sorry not habits but when somebody does something, you know, you focus on that behavior, not on the bad behavior, and you get more of the good behavior. Now this will apply to yourself because I went through and I still do where I could barely get out of bed, I was so depressed with what was going on in my lawyers and divorce, and the people around me, I could not get out of bed. And, I was laying there and this is how you get out of that, this is how...

when you're on the playing field if you're into sports, or you're in a bad relationship that you want different, or your sales – that's what we're learning today, is business. You sit there and you think about all the good things that you have in your life and you be thankful for them, because what happens then, and this is proven, and you don't – what you might want to do is test it. You walk into a room or a party or even with your – anybody around you and you start talking about everything that's wrong with the world, and I don't suggest you do this, you could also do this by the way – put a plant in one room, put a child in one room, put another child in another room, go into that thing, start yelling at that plant, tell them everything that's wrong, everything that's bad, now, if you'd hooked up those lectoids that the scientists have, or even under a microscope, because that plant has atoms inside of it, and inside of us is DNA.

We have – we're programmed. Right now, think about it, what's happening? Automatically you're breathing. Automatically your brain is working, some of you guys' brains are. Automatically your hair is growing – there is a universal force, there's a DNA code inside of you, so you could hook me up, hook up a plant, you could just see it too, hook up a child and go in there, talk negatively, you can even put something on you where you can see your facial expression, you're going to wrinkle more, you're going to look older, feel older, your energy is going to change. Now you walk into – there's a child in this room and this room and you just tell them – you don't even have to say what's bad with them, you say what's bad with yourself, you say what's bad with the world, of the weather – go into this room and you talk about, yeah, there's a storm outside, isn't it beautiful? It's really not a clear nice day, isn't it wonderful that everything's being nourished, fed, isn't it incredible? New York City just went through the most horrific thing in the entire world, was it the bombing of the buildings, right? Well do you know what else happened? We got to show who we were as Americans, and you guys got to show who you were, the Canadians, the Germans, we got to show and we got to feel, and we got to wake up and see how many people came together, and see how many any people now are focused on peace. Focused on helping, I mean, I don't know anything that could've gotten more people together and got to show more people what they were made of and you could feel better and more excited, that yeah, our world is going to change, there are some people out there that are nasty. And, but there are more people out there that are not, so in your business, in whatever you're endeavoring, whatever you're doing whether again you're a restaurant or gas station attendant or anything like that, people walk into your center wherever you're at, whatever store you have, whatever's in your home, and they can feel what's going on, some people you walk into their home, you don't want to stay. You sit next to them, they're taking to you about buying a car, talking to you aboutselling real estate, talking to you about getting your business, and you've got a stomach ache when you're near them and you don't want to talk to them. You don't even want to – it's something horrible, you walk down the street and you glance at somebody and they look mean and nasty and you look away. What happens when you're walking down the street and somebody has a big, huge smile, and they just radiate.

Have you ever seen somebody just radiate? Where they just like, geez, I just want to be around that person. That's what you can become. So how do you do this?

90 % of that is coming from you, and there's a law of attraction and I am so disorganized that I forgot my magnets, but picture magnets, they repel and they can draw. You can set up a whole energy force, where, and you'll have to get better and better where your eyes look different, your smile looks different, your body language is different, and it's a fact, I've seen people like this, not feeling well, like jeez, I'm not buying anything from them, or they're pushing, in your face, and you know they're not telling you the truth. You can tell that, you can tell when your kid's lying.

You need to develop that inside of you. What you will be doing then, what's happening now is that you'll be attracting things that you need. Everybody says, is this magic? Some new age thing? Wait a minute, your body right now is circulating, your cells right now are reproducing, they've proven cancer and all these different things, if you can change your attitude, you can change what your body is being flooded with. Animals can smell fear, we can smell it, I can smell it, I could see it, I could feel it. So you've got to put out this thing, I'm telling you, it'll double and triple your business, because you'll start drawing people to you. I was always fighting with everybody because you know, they were wrong, and I had a friend once say to me, you know, what you're saying is absolutely right, what you're saying could double and triple my business and change my life forever, but I can't hear you because of your tone of voice. You're saying it like you're stupid and you're saying it like you know everything.

And that's true. You've got to know how to get things across without beating somebody up, and that goes for kids, right? It goes – I'm like, what happens if I see you're about to fall in the fire? I've got to yell at you, and they said, yeah, but I think I would've gotten it before I got to that point, had you said it maybe in a different way, because as soon as I heard your voice shrieking, as soon as I saw your face – because I just got so intense. If you come over to my family at Thanksgiving, I had a friend over and he's like, jeez, why is everybody yelling, and I said, we're not yelling, we're discussing. Yeah, because we're passionate and you do want that passion but you don't want it to be negative, you want it to be – think about what you say before you say it, think about you know, before telling somebody what they're doing wrong, list all the things that they're doing right, reinforce that and then say hey, on this avenue, you might want to think about doing this. You might want to think about the fact – then say, what do you think about that or do you think I'm wrong? That's the best thing you can say. Do you think I'm wrong? What do you think? Why are you doing it this way? And they'll go on to give you a list and the first thing I want to do is jump in there, their argument, let them talk, and then you say, so you're telling me that you're not recognizing anyone in your group, anyone in your restaurant, um, because you don't have any time. And you don't have enough energy because you're running around doing something else. Okay. I don't really understand that. We've learned and I have proven to you and you accept the fact that recognition is the number one most important thing so I would think you'd run in there and say whoever sells the most wine tonight, whoever has the highest sales tonight, we're going to honor you on Friday and you're going to be able to have a drink with us, eat with us. Then he's like, no no no, I've got to do this and that, okay, I used my mentor all the time, Jim Rome, you come to me and you tell me your restaurant's about ready to go out of business, I give you the number one thing that's been proven in the world to change your business, and that's recognition, and you don't apply it.

Okay, what's the definition of insanity? Doing the same thing over and over and over again, expecting a different result. You know, when I was playing baseball, when I was playing tennis and now I'm playing golf, they say your swing is wrong and I wasn't doing what I wanted to do, your swing is wrong. You know, so what am I going to do? Swing the same way harder? No, I've got to reprogram, then I've got to get it right, I've got to say, okay, watch me, is this right, and that's what I did in my sales, I taped myself – I have told everybody, I've been in my own business now for 8 years. I have the original phone call that I made, and it is hilarious. One – I – all of you guys by the way should have that original tape. On one of those things I think I burped. I made the sale.

More often than not, I did not make the sale, even when I was in real estate, even when I was a waitress, whatever I was selling, even when I was a kid, I sold because they wanted me. I sold myself, and that's what you need to do. You need to sell yourself, okay? And you need to change what's going on in your body, you need to feed – 90 % of it is going to be your mind, so guess what you should be doing 90 % of the time? Reading. Listening to tapes. That's the difference. Somebody was over at my house and they had been in the same business I've been in for 22 years, and was still not even close to making $10,000 let alone what I'm making after three years. About 4-5 of them were looking around this beautiful house on the water in Florida, and all my toys and all my fun stuff, and me who's in shorts, who really doesn't speak proper English, who has never had an education, um, and they're like, you know we were trying to put our finger on what it is and why you were able to do what you're doing and we don't, and we've got it – it's your energy. We know about you, we know who you are, we know what you've done, I still didn't get it, then I'm around you and I feel good. I feel like whatever it is you're doing, I want to do, whatever it is you're teaching, I want to hear. Then what happened when I said I don't know if that's really it, I'm not always the most likeable person, I always don't get along with people, I really, um, I'm alone a lot... reading... by myself, and he said, what? I said I read and... listen to tapes, about five hours a day.

There was a big box. He grabbed the box and he pulled it over, he said this is it. This is the reason why. And um, it was a box full of books. It was a box full of tapes, books that dated back, you know, 1925, when was Think and Grow Rich written? Look at the copyright. It's got the same facts that you're learning now. What year? 1937.

And what happens though is that when we're young, what are you told? You're up on the fence, balancing around and you're like – what does your mom say? You're going to fall! Ah! You know, but you are programmed to succeed, you are programmed to do anything you want to do. I don't want to go out and be a violinist, I don't have the talent for it and I've never wanted that. When you have a dream inside your head, it's because you can't accomplish that, you wouldn't have that... if you didn't – if you couldn't and you didn't have it inside of you.

So again, here's the thing I carry with me, what's in here, books, tapes, more books, more tapes, and my purse that I carry everywhere which feels like a million zillion pounds, and I'm never really sure what's in here because I throw stuff in here and stuff, but... mostly they're just tapes. And, books. And real quickly, write this down, you guys, when I'm telling you to do something, I expect if you're really really serious about wanting things to change, and wanting to be successful – I would think, and this is my thought, I don't want to just be successful and just realize my dreams – I want to do it in the least amount of time and the easiest way, okay? You know that story about the fly. I see this so often, there's – have you ever watched it inside your house? There's a fly and this fly is trying to get outside, and there's an open window right here but he's hitting this sliding glass door, and this guy is working hard, he is just hitting it and hitting it and hitting it, I'm like why doesn't he just go over there. Stand back, feel the air and move over there. What I'm trying to tell you here is it's not – just like the restaurant owner, just like some of my real estate friends. Just like if somebody owns a McDonalds or a convenience store or whatever I don't care if you work 20 hours. If it's – I can do in one hour what that person is doing in 20 and so can you. You can even do more if you make these changes. IF you teach yourself, you can learn it, okay? Because I was that fly, it was like jeez, this isn't working, I've got to do more. It's like excuse me, it's not working. Step back, find out what you're doing that's different from the people that are going through that window.

Okay? We're not flies. We're smarter than that. Don't, if you're working as hard you can, or if you're going for a goal and you want to be the best tennis player in the world, if you've got a wrong grip and you're just practicing it over and over, or a wrong swing in golf or a wrong mindset in business and you just keep it up, what's going to happen? It can be like that fly that just dies. So if you're doing something, and it's not working, that's why I've asked everyone to tape themselves. Can you imagine if the day that you started, you taped yourself, then all of the sudden, you're now making a million dollars, and you can give that tape to people now that you're trying to help so they can believe it, you guys would never believe that I was you know, from a small town on a farm earning $10 an hour and made a million dollars by my third year.

It's hard to believe but you watch those old videos and you can believe it. I don't know if it would be as powerful if you didn't have those original things or if people would relate to you as much. To this day, I hear, you have the jewelry, you have the car, the house, you have the clothes, you can speak in front of people, of course you're going to get all this, everything you touch turns to gold. Let me show you what it used to be like, and you can't always tell. You've got to have these pictures, some people would never believe that I used to weigh 180 pounds, that I could never get up in front of an audience and not pass out. Or, I just, you know? And also you can listen to yourself and you can, jeez, that was horrible. And you can see your growth, and you can see your accomplishments, like, I'm going to tie this together now, you wake up in the morning and you're depressed and you feel bad, and all this bad stuff has happened, and it's hard not to focus on it because people are calling you and you're getting something in the mail or somebody's really really, you know, like when you're going to break up, it really screwed you, and it's hard not to be depressed, so what do you do? If you don't feel well enough to even get out of bed and you don't feel confident enough to go out and make that sales' call, and you don't feel your best, what do you do?

That's what I was like, oh yeah, motivate me right, I can't get out of bed. So I read this in a book, be, give thanks. I don't have anything to be thankful for? Jim Rome said, well, the only thing worst than what's happening to you is you could be ugly. I was telling him this is happening to me, I can't do this, I can't go out and create new things, we all do that. My child has – something's wrong with my child, I did this training in Tennessee, that I knew in that room that there was a woman who just had found out that her child had been molested by another colleague of hers'. Okay, and she was there and she'd done $20,000 – how did $20,000 personal sales, how could she do that? It was because of the way she was programmed, she was so blessed that her child had not been killed, she gave thanks. She was so blessed that she caught it and it didn't go on. I mean this is tough. This is tough, I didn't have that to deal with and I was ashamed I could even be depressed. We had a woman in a wheelchair that was earning over $8,000 a month. And her mother had just died, and I said, what are you doing here? She's like, hey, my mom had a good life because I had enough money to care for her for the last year of her life, and I'm here, I've got my children here because I want them to learn the values and I want them to learn, even if they only get 1 %, that's 1 % more, and the next time they hear something, they're going to get a little bit more. And the next time somebody does something crappy to you, you can say jeez, this isn't as bad as it could be, so I was laying there and I thought, okay, what am I thankful for. Well, I have that stinky little dog that loves me no matter what happens, she's been kissing me and I'm like, okay, and I've got a little bitty tiny smile, thankful for my little dog.

Then all of the sudden I started feeling this energy pouring into me. Oh my goodness, how ridiculous is this situation? When I worked at Boeing and I lived in just a piece of crap home, and drove a car that would barely, you know, it was so embarrassing and you know, now, I have this. You know, now I have this, I have my health, I have you know, my parents, a lot of my parents aren't even alive, it's just amazing, and you start giving thanks and something strange comes over you, again, I actually felt my whole entire body relax, then I started feeling something else, and I'm pretty sure that I'm not a chemist or anything but it's either called endorphins or serotonin was being released. I'm like, jeez this is ridiculous, get out of bed, and I did this before I first started my business. I went to a training where these people were on stage, talking about how much money they were making, showing me their houses, it really depressed me.

I, um went home thinking, ugh, what am I going to do? You know? I have a husband that's mean to me, berating me, laughing at me, my friends think I'm insane, I can't do it. These people had somebody mentoring them, these people got in at the ground floor, these people were doing this and these people were doing that and this person you know, had connections, I don't have any of that. These people have 20 years on me and I'm just starting out, I should've got in 20 years ago, again… I need some help here then something that Jim Rome once said, I have forever in my heart, every single time I go there, I want to change my neurons, I want to change my DNA, I want to change what's happening to me. For things to change, you have to change. I thought that was the stupidest thing I've ever heard in my life. My ex-husband or my husband at that time was drinking, he was doing drugs, he was mentally and physically beating me up, he has to change, not me.

You know? He has to stop that. Same with the lawyers, these lawyers need to stop it, it's not fair and they need to stop. I want you to get that book, Who Moved my Cheese. Everybody. Get it when you leave, okay? Read it in an hour, go get that book. Um, so I was thinking, that doesn't make any sense. So the next time he started to get verbally abusive, I said, I'm leaving. I'm not going to listen, I'm not going to allow you to talk to me like that, I'm leaving, and I walked out the door. And I came back in a couple hours and then um, I have some people the other day, we were on a phone call, I made a suggestion and he said that's the stupidest thing I've ever heard in my life. I said, you know, I really appreciate your input but I would really appreciate it if you didn't put me down and try to make me look really really bad, and I will try to get better ideas in the future. Normally what I would've said is, you – or somebody help me. No, I'm going to help myself. And it didn't work when I got louder, it didn't work – you know how sometimes a bully will push you around, all of the sudden you have to hit them and he'll leave you alone, or you know, unfortunately when I was a kid, they beat me up. You've got to be able to change a little bit – sometimes you need to push back, but the way you do it, guess what happened on that call, there was like 20 people on that call, that guy looked really bad. Now if I would've said, just tell him he's this and he's that, and that's what I would too because that's all I knew, that's what they told me to do. That's what the book said, don't react, say hey, that's not the fact really, and I just think I'm deserving of manners, and I will treat you this way and you want to do it instantly by the way. I also said something good about him, I said you've helped me on a lot of things and I really appreciate it and you have so much value, I hope to one day have as much value, I just thought this was a good idea. It was amazing, he looked like a jerk. And my point was made, and that's what you've got to do – these are skills.

These are relationship skills and you're in the relationship skills business. If you're trying to work at home, you're trying to own your own business, you're trying to be different than everyone else, you have got to learn the skills, okay? So and there are tons of books out there, you know I do a training, very first training because everyone says to me, you got lucky or you're not telling us something, or you're doing something that is illegal or you have a secret. I said you know what, I do have a secret, and it's this – I hold up my library card. I could not afford Zig Ziggler, Tony Robbins, I couldn't afford to go to a seminar, I couldn't afford when I was 12 years old to figure out and go to a baseball camp, my parents couldn't afford for me to take private tennis lessons, so guess what's in those buildings, 1920-something they wrote that book, thousands of books from thousands of successful people, from tennis champions to public speaking to any single thing you want and it's free, okay?

Then I hear this. I don't have time to read. I was like, you don't have time to read because you don't read, if you had time to read you'd read a time management book. And it's true, one minute management is excellent. I have a book and I have an audio cassette where I make a few sacrifices. Do I like to watch TV? Yes. Do I like to listen to music on the radio? Absolutely. But I wanted to get over and through the success so I could listen to and watch as much TV as I wanted, I could drive and go anywhere I wanted, I could golf anywhere I wanted and I wanted to get it done, so I instead when I was first broke and first dying, I spent 90 % of my time learning. Every single time you got in my car, there was a tape. In that cassette, or a CD, every single time, and I had to listen to stuff over and over again. To this day, I will pick up Think and Grow Rich, read it – and think, I must have read that book about 20 times and now because I've changed, because I'm a little bit different, because my brain neurons have changed ,my cells have changed ,my everything, I'm reading these words as if, wow, I never read that! All of the sudden, I'm absorbing more, getting more, I'll read them over and over. Sometimes it's like this is not good, this is falling apart, grab a book and I just open it – guess what, the answer is right there. Man, that was wild. Because they're basic basic answers you could open them almost anywhere and read something and it will tell you you know, you need to focus on being thankful, you need to start changing your energy, then all of the sudden, thoughts – what do you think Einstein and what do you think me, you, anyone has an idea comes from? Where does it come from? It's got to come from somewhere, right? Who cares? You've got to be open for it, you've got to be on the same – you can go tune into that, so that nobody can – no matter what religion you are, because everybody in this room believes that there are radio waves right now running across from me. And TV, um, waves, okay, how are we videotaping that? You could see me on the screen back there, something in the air, right? Is that true? It's not magic, it's not evil.

There's also thoughts going in the air. You can

develop to where you can pick up different thoughts, and if you don't believe that you walk into a room where everybody is nasty, and everybody is mean – I used to go into prisons because I was a court reporter. You go in there man, you just have this feeling, this thing in the back of your neck, it's called instinct, you were born with it. It's the thoughts, you feel it. Then you walk into a church, what do you feel? Calm, peace. So you can tap into those things and you can feel them and you can change, and you can ask for questions and your subconscious is so powerful. I just can't find anything and I'm like okay, I want to know where this is at, I've got to find my passport. That's actually what happened, I was just losing it, I couldn't find my passport anywhere. And, um, I said to my subconscious and I had read this, I didn't really believe – I said, tell me where my passport is, I want to know. Go out and find it and come back to me and tell me. I woke up in the morning and I remembered that I had a rip in my purse and the passport had fallen through the rip and there was the passport, very very cool. Okay, so – you don't know the answer to something, they're in the books, there's people that are out there people that can help you and for things to change, you have to change, don't – if somebody, you know, like the corporation that you're in with, if they're not doing the thing you want – if you read that book Who Moved my Cheese? You'll understand what you need to do. I did not like the way the focus of the training that I was getting. I felt like people weren't telling the truth, I felt they were hiding things, I felt like, you've been in this business, you've been in – owning your own business for 20 years, and I made in six months, I'd not want to listen to you. I want only the top people because by the way, I could learn from somebody that came in yesterday, because I didn't do $20,000 last month, I didn't do that in sales.

Mostly I don't care to do it anymore.

I did it – I would sure as heck try to find what that person is doing, I try to get into what that person is doing, I test it, and I go on.

[presentation continues]

I just believe that at the end of today, just with what you've just leaned, with your thoughts, that you can magnetize things to you, you can magnetize people, you can magnetize ideas, you can ask – I don't believe in coincidences, I'm here in Australia, you guys are here in this room, I believe that we're changing the world, I believe that we're talking about the world, we're talking about caring, love, success, abundance, and some of the rest of the world is talking about recession. I think that's hilarious. No, we can change the energy, we can change by, I mean how many people are we going to effect today? Not just with what will happen today. You could be walking through a mall or a town or anything and have a book in your hand that says Think and Grow Rich, and you might not even know that somebody sitting around notices your book and even though they don't say anything, guess what they might do. Guess what I would do? I would dig up one of my Think and Grow Rich books – that was one of the best books I've ever read.

By her having that book might've changed and made me a better speaker because I haven't dug that out for years, so I'm going to do that. So, the other question I get, and I think a lot of people need help on, and what is very important, what I'm teaching you here, this is just like huge, and they'll say, you know, I went to um, and I listened to your training tape and I went to go see Tony Robbins, I read this incredible book, Think and Grow Rich, and I just walked out of seeing Tony Robbins and I was so hyped up, so excited, how do I keep that alive? This is huge you guys – how do I get my sales staff, my staff, how do I get them to go in there, okay? And you keep it alive by you becoming a Tony Robbins, you becoming the excitement, you keeping it alive within yourself. Now, how do I keep it alive? How do I keep going? How do I not get depressed? How do I get not angry when somebody rips down my advertising or sends me a nasty message or whatever? I'm getting better and better because I have spent more time developing it within me.

I don't look outside, I take it, you should be listening to those tapes and videos, the reason why you lose that momentum, energy and feeling is for the same reason that you would if you all of a sudden stopped eating right. Why am I gaining weight? Well, when you were losing weight, what were you doing? I was eating good foods, I was drinking a lot of water, I was exercising, now I'm eating crummy foods – you've got to do it everyday! Some people don't get that. If you guys could just get that, every single day before you get out of bed, you've got to get a book into your hands. That's what you guys miss – I don't have time.

Get up a half an hour earlier. In your car, have a tape, make the time, if you really really want your life to be different. Um, have the books and this is funny but it's true, in the bathroom. You know? If you're studying and you want to be the best and have the best life and you want to – always be reinforcing, you know, and you obviously don't want to be listening to – watch what you're reading, if you're in there reading things that – I know that when I read, somebody gave me a novel because I love Anthony Hopkins the actor and they gave me the novel Hannibal. Jeez, all of the sudden I was afraid like I'm not going to read this, this is poisoning me, I'm scared – thinking – and I'm focusing on, you know, and during when I was court reporting I did a lot of rape cases, muggings – why is it that somebody is, you know, and they asked the rapist, why did you pick this woman? They said because I saw the way they walked, I saw the way they stood, the way they had no confidence, and I knew it would be easy. What do you think a con man does? He sees your vulnerability; you've got to work on that, see that so you don't attract that anymore.

Some of you guys are attracting shysters into your business, right? You're attracting whiners. My people on my sales force, even when I was head waitress, they did not mess with me, this is the way it is and this is what you want to do, I'm going to love you if you don't do it but leave me alone and don't take my time. If they ask a question that you know is in the manual, you know it's in the video, you've known that they've heard. What do you do when your child comes to you and they say, how do you spell this? You show them how to use a dictionary.

What do you when a kid comes to you and says, can I have $20, I want to buy this. You should be saying great, you know what, we've just started a home based family business, we've just started a new restaurant, we've just started a valet service, a new real estate company – I want you to go deliver 1,000 of these announcements of our grand opening. Okay? You know Sam Walton? Do you guys have like a Waltons? It's like a K-Mart – they started small, they had their children out doing things to earn money, okay? They have – they have and they put and they teach – some of you guys are trying to manage, you're trying to do everything for somebody, and you're trying to give them too much. You say, you've only got to do two things the first week you're in. You've got to understand what you're selling, you've got to understand your product, your marketplace. You've got to know what's out there for sale, see what you've got – you've got to know that product forword and backward so you are confident, and you've got to see the best points in there so that when you talk about this, the people are just like jeez, and this is what happens to me – I've had so many people say to me, I have no idea what you're talking about, all I know is that whatever you're doing, I want to be part of. It really – you will hear that on my tapes, you will hear a live sales call, where the woman says, I don't know what you're doing, I don't know what you said, but whatever it is, I want to buy it. Okay, do you have that?

I don't know what it is but whatever it is, I want to buy it. Okay, and you've got to believe that you are in the best business that there is, that you – that's another thing – you've got to love what you do, if you don't love what you do, find what you love, and there's different aspects, you know, some people would open up a restaurant, they love to cook, that's what they're good at, that's where they should be – they don't love to do advertising, then you find somebody that works with you that loves to do advertising, okay, and also you can also find places for people sometimes, when they're not doing what they should do, what do you love? What do you love, why did you choose this? And this is what you focus on, okay, and you'll develop those skills and get those skills, again, they're going to be in the libraries books, videos you're going to see, people you talk to. The money will come. I also believe and I know that most of you guys do, is whenever you lie or um, take advantage of somebody or – it's really hard to remember the lie, and it's – just so much easier to know that you're going to mess up.

I was telling you guys the other day where I felt like the worst person in the world because I had a deal fall through, I had a girlfriend who lost a big commission on a real estate deal, fell through. I'm like Karen, you should have so many deals on the burner that you don't care, that you're onto the next one, you should have so many salespeople, so many clients, so many customers that if you know, you're giving the best service, doing the best and every single aspect and you're following through that it doesn't matter because some people, you have to say look, I mean I've been on the phone where they're questioning, I'm like, hey, it sounds like it's not for you. Okay? I've got a lot of people that are ready and willing, why don't you think about it, I've got to go. They say wait wait, I say I've got to go – call me back when you're serious, I'm going to go out and get more clients. Again, that's through advertising.

Another thing is I – the reason why I went so fast, is because I did more advertising than anyone else. Was not a better sales person, I got better because I did more, um, I couldn't afford to put big ads, I couldn't afford to um, take out commercials, I couldn't afford to do billboards but I could afford to make up little handwritten cards. I had a 22 year old kid that came to me, he's the girlfriend of one of my assistants and he works on my jet skis, my little boat, he's incredible, a good looking kid. 16, he had to take care of his parents because they were crack cocaine addicts, I think by 17 he had bought his first house. So he came to me, he said I want to start a business of boat cleaning where I want to start a business of boat cleaning where I'm my own business man, I don't have to work for somebody else, do you want to go into business with me? He was really asking me to give him some money to start him up. I said sure, sure. I said how bad do you want it? I want it really bad. Okay, it was Friday, I said tonight we're going to go to the computer and make a flyer about you working on boats and we're going to go out to every house on the ocean that has a boat and we're going to slip it into their mailbox. *I'm going out tonight, I'm going partying with my buddies.*

I said, see you. So, that's what you do with anyone you're trying to work with, anyone you're trying to motivate. They've got to motivate themselves. You can give them the skills, there are too many people out there, you have to say, my time, my energy, my care, is reserved for the people that are serious. Do you think successful people sit around and you know, no. You were lucky. How many times have you heard top people, Trump and Bill Gates, the harder I work, the luckier I get. I worked hard. I didn't get lucky, I worked hard, and now I get to play and I got it over with, I didn't drag it out, and now I get to tell everybody off if I want to, I get to do whatever I want. It's just, I have – I have such a different life now. And, when people made fun of me and put me down – my very first generation piece had me on the front with my car – I didn't have a house, it had a Porsche on the front. Somebody took that because they were so upset and so jealous and um, it was in the same business I'm in and mailed it into the Porsche dealer.

I got a letter from the Porsche dealer saying, we will sue you if you do not take this off the cover. I couldn't believe it. And I raged and I cried and lost all my energy, after throwing a tizzy fit, a tantrum, I was laying down, feeling sorry for myself, and I should've done – but I hadn't learned it yet. I should've said, okay, what is that saying, you get lemons, you make lemonade? So I said fine, I'm going to buy the biggest and greatest house in the world and own it, and I'm going to put that on the cover. And I did, and guess what happened? Sales triples. I went up to that guy, because I made Porsche tell me who it was. [laughter] And I thanked him for tripling my business.

Just met this really really great guy and he owns his own valet company, we're sitting here talking, he's only 30 and I've got to get ready to go, we stand up and his knees just about give out, and he said, oh I have to run all day long, I said what are you doing? Why are you parking the cars? I don't understand, you're more valuable, why aren't you going out getting more business? He says, I've got to make sure things run right. I said no, you've got to get the right people in there to run that right so that you can go state wide, then you can go nation-wide, what do you think, Mr. Hurst is in the storefront? You think, you know, Mr. Gates is down there working on every single computer, making sure everyone's working on the computer? He did when he started, and that's what some of you guys are doing. You're enabling your people. Your job is to not constantly be standing – your job is to empower them, just like it is your kids, to let them stand on their own, to train them and teach them to be leaders so that you have duplication, I'm like, you've got to think bigger, why just be in Palm Beach? Go throughout the whole state, go into the next state. How can I possibly do that? You have to have the leaders in place – I have never been to Australia, how the heck did I have all you guys where I'm getting paid on you guys? Never met you,

you know, I was out on the ocean, I fell off my jet ski, I'm laying on my back, thinking, jeez, I'm making $3,000 an hour right now. And I'm not running around – Mr. Hurst is not down at that counter.

You've got to delegate, and yeah they're going to mess up, and actually his partner, this morning I called him and said, you won't believe Australia, he said hey I know you're doing a big training today, and my friends have a story for you to tell, he said, so I think he'll be perfect for you, you know, he goes – he hadn't heard it yet, so the guy gets on the phone and he said there's this little boy, he walks into this big store, he asks the store manager, hey can I use your phone, over there, I've got to make a phone call, and he says sure and the little kid can't reach the phone and the guy thought, I should help him out, then he forgot about him.

Later the kid figures it out and brings in this huge crate, gets up on the crate and calls, said hey, you know, my name is Tim, and I cut lawns and um, you know, I understand that you're getting your lawn cut, for $35 I'll do it for less. And she said, the woman said, well I'm really happy with the person that I have, he said, well I'll tell you what, with the $35, I'll also rake your leaves, and the woman on the phone said, well, you know what, my guy already does that. He says, okay, for $35 an hour, I'll trim all your bushes, I'll pick up all the garbage, I mean for $35 I'll also do that, and she said you know what, I'm really really happy with what I'm doing right now. So then the little kid hangs up.

The store guy goes, jeez, um, I'll give you a job! And the kid goes, I've already got a job, I was just doing follow-up. Do you understand what that is? The follow-up is so important, the follow-up with your managers are important, and you can also coordinate this to the military, you know, you have generals and you build generals and you're looking for those because you cannot possibly be here in Sydney and also be in Florida, okay? I have not even met the people that I make money off who live in – I've never been to Wisconsin, I've got a huge check coming out of there – Mr. Hurst has probably never been to – Mr. McDonald, they've probably never been to every McDonalds store, and yeah, you're going to have some issues come up, you're going to have – if you own a chain, everywhere, you're going to have some difficulties come up, so you're going to go over and get the right tools into those managers' hands, and that's another thing, these tools, the videos that I want you guys to start taping yourselves the audios that you make, these are tools – do you understand how this whole thing happened? How did I know to take my very first call?

I didn't, I read a book on, you know, you want to listen to your calls because then you can re-evaluate yourself. So I did that accidentally, well, I didn't know what was going to happen. What happened to me that I was so overwhelmed, and I was so sick and tired of telling every single person the same thing over and over, I thought how am I going to get $40,000 people underneath me if I have to talk to every single one of them?

How am I going to open up these little mini-me's?

That's a good one. All around the entire world, how does Mr. Hurst do it, how do these people do it? They get the training. You can't possibly – if you want to have a lot of money with the least amount of work, I give them a tape. I couldn't do it, I would've had a break-down, I would've burned myself out, I couldn't do it so I taped myself and I got that into those peoples' hands – and, that's what these people do, they duplicate themselves without being the issue, but using technology and using tools – if you do not do that, you might become a really good one restauranteur – Clogote Bankers is a big realtor over in the US, there's tons of big realtors, but there's also tons of little bitty mom and pops things – mom and pop work and use just as much hours as that big one that has a bunch of mini-me's everywhere, and so for the same amount of work, the same amount of time, the same amount of energy, you can have a little tiny thing in your back yard or you could become gigantic and you could be making your telephone sales calls, doing your training videos, for your sales, all around the world – from a yacht. Instead of from a broken down chair and apartment that smells, which is what I was doing. Okay? So, you have got to think differently and you've got to be open, and you've got to listen and you've got to learn. It's not hard, it can be fun – what's hard is working so much time and running and having your knees give out and your back give out because you're working so hard but you didn't work smart.

You've all got the same amount of time. What's the difference between me and Trump? What's the difference between this and that? It's usually, they're doing more in less amount of time and energy, and they know more. So, whatever you – if you're happy where you're at, I don't think you would be here. If you want to realize your dreams, you can. It's there, it's programmed, you wouldn't have that dream, so now you've got to learn how to do it, and if you can't do the action because for some reason it's just like jeez, I don't know what it is, I know what to do but I just keep screwing up. Do you all do that? So how do you need to fix that? You need to re-read and re-listen, every single day.

Even, you know, and it's not like a big thing, it makes you feel great, and everyone's like, I don't want to do every single thing everyday. Do you eat everyday? Do you go to the bathroom? Breathe everyday? It's automatic, you just do it.

[presentation continues]

You know, the clapping, you guys put your hand on your heart, feel, what is that? You feel a heartbeat? Do you know the clapping is the same as tribal, aborigines, the Indians, the drum beats, again it's because of energy, it just does something to you when you hear, you've got to get that inside of you. The other thing with promotions and with investing and everybody's asking me all the time, what do you invest in, especially with the stock market the way it is, real estate. I invest in my business, I put my money back into my business. The reason why I was more successful is that I didn't just talk to my friends and family. I understood very very quickly that it was about advertising and no matter how bad you are, you get better and better, so in order for me to be able to compete with someone that's been in 20 years with somebody that's already established, I've got to do more advertising. I couldn't do more advertising because I was broke. Did I let that use as an excuse? No. I got up and went out, and every time I got in my car, I made it a goal just to put out one thing.

And then, guess what happened, I was such positive feedback because um, I just, you know, every single time, I'm in the car, everywhere I go, my goal is to just put out – you want to make every single thing count so that you're not burned out, you're not tired, and you just do it naturally. You just naturally are advertising your business 24/7. What does a jeweler do? Do you think that they're wearing crummy jewelry? No. They're wearing and they're looking the part and people are asking them, oh my goodness – that's what happens to you, I get people all the time saying, without me saying – it's just me talking. What kind of business are you in? There it is. Okay.

There was something this morning that I put out, um, gosh my mind went blank, but the training is on there this morning on what he was saying to them The other thing that you want to realize is, somebody in this room, somebody listening, is going to do it if you don't. Is going to get out there and contact – those people that have fences.

They're going to get out there and get into the papers. Because you dropped your pipeline of advertising, and I would not let them do that – somebody else is going to talk to your friends and family, you know, again, my realtor friend had a cousin and she never told him she was a realtor, and he bought a $10 million dollar house from somebody else. I'm like, why don't they understand? Why don't they know you've got your own business? That's the difference between why that guy made the sale and you didn't. Now you got it – then a guy friend of mine, I saw him a month later, I said did you ever get that letter out? No. I said, are you working today? No, it's really slow today.

No wonder! You can generate and create and double and triple with even hardly any effort by making letting everyone know that you are in business. I got my thing right here, on my pen. This is my business on here. Um, you know, I wear and dress and look at all times like I'm in business. And um, you have got to leave a trail everywhere you go, you don't have to get in peoples' faces, it's the best when they are asking you, jeez, why are you so happy? Where did you get your energy? How did you get to to go on that vacation? There it is. Also if you listen, you're in the grocery store, you're in – shopping for Christmas right now, everybody's out and about, you listen – everybody's going to be telling you and you're going to be hearing the conversations in elevators and on escalators and everywhere you go, in restaurants, oh man, I wish I had a little bit more money this year. I wish I had more energy, I don't have enough energy to even do this. I don't have – and you should have something on you that says, listen, if you want things to change, I can help you out, give me a call, I'm a professional helper outer. But um, the other reason why I beat all sales records – I had these skills, remember I beat out the babysitter, I beat out the realtors, even when I was waiting tables. I did more numbers than anyone.

And, I remember going to my Grandpa, I wanted to – I loved to play baseball and I wanted to try out for the team – I was the youngest and smallest person, in fact, you didn't even try out until you were in the top grade, right? I mean these girls were huge, and I said, um, that I was afraid, he said, well, what are you strengths? And I said, I can really hit the ball, I'm really a good hitter but I'm not very good at picking up grounders, but I can catch, as long as it doesn't hit in front of me – I was actually dyslexic so I would move the wrong way and I didn't even know that then. And I couldn't run very fast, I just was not a fast runner. He said, okay, what you want to do, is you want to focus – and – on your strength. You want to make that even stronger. Since you love it and you're good at it but you don't want to ignore your weakness. Spend 90 % on your strength, spend some time on your weaknesses. So he would take me out, throw grounders to me – same when I first started my business, I was not a good political person, I was not a good talker, I was not a good speaker, that was my weakness, but I figured I could make up for it – remember, I was the mad advertiser leaver I would go out at midnight, only because so nobody would see me, and I would put my little advertisings everywhere. One time I went out – you guys know this story, my ex-husband had disconnected the car, and it was raining, I was in Seattle, and I went back, just started bawling, and I said, I can't do this – what am I going to do? And I had a bike, and I thought I'm not going to ride my bike in the rain, then I sat with myself, do you want to be number one? Do you want to live like this the rest of your life? This is the difference between being mediocre and being... successful, are you going to do what it takes? Is it that big a deal to ride your bike in the rain? Is it that big a deal to get up a half an hour earlier to get you where you want to be – so I put those stupid things in my backpack and I went out in the rain and I rode my bike and I got my advertising out there. And I did more than anyone else, and I went faster than anyone else, and with each call, I got better, and I got more ideas. With each book I read – because you know, do not wait, do not say to yourself, I'm not going to do this until I'm reading every single day and until you know, the weather clears, I'm not going to do any of this until I get a desk, a bank open – just go. You know? Just get out there because it takes a while to get that snowball effect and just like, are you going to go right into a golf tournament, right into a cricket tournament? No. What are you going to do? You're going to practice and practice, so my big strength was, I could hit. And, then he said over his shoulder anyway, hit it over the fence and you can walk the bases. I was like, man... that's true!

So what I did was, I hit it over the fence by getting out ten times more advertising than anyone else, and the one thing that you do have when you're broke usually is time, you don't have any money but you do have time. You do. If you think about how much time – and by the way, if you don't, it's because you're giving away your time. You're not doing quality. When I get somebody on the phone and they're going on and on and on about their problems, I am not helping them by letting them talk about things that are wrong. I will interrupt somebody and say, hey you got anything good to say? You got anything that went right today? You've got, you know, do you have both arms and both legs? Can you hear? Because I've got people that can't hear. I've got a blind guy that's funner to be with than you and he's got some problems. Then they want to get off the phone. Do not let people do that to you. If you don't have time, it's because of what you've done and it's how you're doing it. For things to change, you've got to change, so all of the sudden, try to figure out where you can get more time. Try to figure out that, maybe having a family day, where you could make it fun, but everybody goes out and we're going to go do this but first we're going to go put out these letters to people that have boards – you can make it fun. You know? Maybe your spouse is like crying all the time that you never have time, you're not romancing – to talking, whatever. Hey, listen to some – audios together. Let's go out and um, get some exercise, you ride the bike and we'll put our new business out, you know? Let's go out and see what other people are doing in advertising. I know a couple, their marriage was not doing well, and they got on bikes, one, they got exercise. If you don't have time to exercise, time to take care of yourself, time to put back into yourself, and time to make extra money, there's a reason why. It's because you're doing the wrong thing – you could look at stuff. I have people that work twelve hours, I have one lady that works all day long, single mother and she's got six children. So how does she find time at a twelve hour job? How do they do it? You've got to figure that one out. You've got to figure that one out, and you've got to work smart. You've got to clean the house, right? It's something you've got to do – you have to make dinner, you have to go to work. Is there some way, that you can have a – something you know, a recorder in your ear where you're listening while you have something, a recorder in your ear where you're listening while you're working. Sometimes you can't, you know? No way. Is there some way that you can turn on the stereo and have these playing over and over while you um, clean the house. Right? Can you wear a walkman to the grocery store?

On your way to work, can you listen to a time management thing? At work, can you start working on yourself by only saying positive things, by every single time you – hear something negative, you say – hey, what happened to you that was good today? You're here. Do you have cancer? Do you have, you know... isn't your mother like in really really good health? Guess what you just did – that person stops, changes the energy, guess what that person's going to do? Let's say it's your boss.

Jeez, that's a good guy, I like having him around, I like being around him. Man I always feel so good about so and so, they're always – man I like to be with them, then guess what they're going to do? What are you doing that's different. I'm reading, I've got this incredible, incredible tape that I'm listening to, This girl called Chris Carley.

There you go! Listen to it. Um, so, you want to do that. And, um, consistency. And you get that consistency just like you would working out, by not, you know, do a little bit and you warm up and you go out and you get stronger and stronger every single day. And we're going to make a new CD and we're going to send it out to people and you can say, you've got to listen to this, but you've got to be the one that's doing it first so that they'll ask you. I do not want you guys ever going to beg for business. People are going to want to know what it is you're doing because you are going to be generating something different when you walk out of here.

You will never be the same person again after today. I don't even care – some people will be ten times different, some peoples' entire life, their check will change, their relationships will change, but I don't care if it's just a tiny tiny bit, that's something that will be different for you and be in the back of your mind for the rest of your life. Now, why am I so passionate about this? I think it's a bunch of crap to work for somebody else, and retire at 65 and have a lifespan of two years. And that is the national worldwide average of a man that works to age 65. And I do not believe that there's going to be social security, I do not believe there's going to be these huge huge companies – they go under all the time. I want to believe in me, the only thing I can control is me.

My gramps retired and got sick and he died. And, he was always saying, he always thought that it was important that he worked for somebody else because that's what he was taught, and if you do that, your stress level, what happens to your body, you miss out on your children being raised, I mean, when you have your own business, and that's another thing is, you do not want to not stop living your life, I want to teach you how to be out playing golf when somebody asks you, what do you do? I own a restaurant, I own a valet service, I own my own business and I work right from home. Well, how can you golf? What's going to happen is, you're going to get that person involved in your business. Let's say you own a valet service, you know what valets are, right? They park cars. Do you know anybody that owns a restaurant that needs a better valet service? Let's say you own a company that's house cleaners – you're playing golf, who do you think is playing golf? People that have money. Who do you think – you think somebody wants to go into business with you or be associated with you if you're all haggard because you're hunched over a computer? I make more money when I'm out having fun, and I'm generating more people buying my services, buying my product, than I am hunched over at home. I do not and I did not when I started, I worked smart.

I hired the kids' neighbors to put stamps on my envelopes, okay? I only had to pay them like $15 for 1,000 – that would take the kid about an hour and a half, two hours – I'm not working for $15 an hour, so if you guys are doing that, you've got to think. Now the dumb thing would be to pay the kid, to pay somebody to come clean your house and then sit around and watch TV. If you would pay yourself $10 an hour to make your bed, then – and you think you're worth more than that, then you need to have somebody do that so that you can go out and do more and that's like, well that doesn't make any sense – I don't even have $10 to put up an ad. That's what I said to myself, I said I'm just going to not make my bed until I can afford it – that's how I lived. It wasn't important. My mom will tell you, she told this story to some of you guys yesterday.

She said I would chase Chris around, her room would be a nightmare, she'd come home from school, I'd see her socks and her pants and shirt, off, she'd be gone, be a little trail. I chased her around saying what do you think, you're going to have a maid some day? I said yes I do, I am going to mother. I can remember my mother, so strange, I had this huge Malibu mansion, she said you know how much it's going to cost to clean those windows? Do you know how long it's going to take you? I said you think I'm going to clean the windows? I feel really proud that I could put in and feed business, an entrepreneur that has started his own window cleaning business. And I'm in there yelling at him, you need to put flyers out, telling everybody about your business, and you have done such a great job, or you are really bad at cleaning windows and there's too many people out there, I don't have to put up with this, I'm getting somebody else because I've got this flyer right here. Any aspect you can do this for. What's going to happen now is I want to know because we're going to have lunch with the top people in this room right now.

I'm going to quiz them, come back and then let you guys know what they're doing. So, I um, we're going to break for lunch but first I want um, to know the highest salespeople here in this room because that's where I'm going to learn what's happening over here, what we can do and how we can do this, and then we're all going to go out, have lunch, and come back, and by the way, you always want to be the top. Because you never, it's just too easy not to – somebody else is going to do it – you've got to think, you're going to see these people, this is what happened to me, I went to this big training and all these people were up there, I did this much, this much, I'm thinking those guys are morons, I should be able to do ten times more than what they do – I'm going to find out what they're doing and I'm going to go out there and do ten times more. That's what you have to do, you have to practice longer, harder.

Somebody also once said to me, that's good that you're doing really well Chris, money was always really really important to you, it's not a big deal to me. I said you are so wrong. Your daughter just had a grand baby that I know that you haven't even gotten to go visit in the last month because you can't afford to get on a plane and go over there. I know that you can't afford the private schools. It's not about money, it's not about having more toys, its' about what you can give and offer and um, experience, um, the lifestyle and what you can... also, I remember somebody said, I'm doing okay, I'm a single guy, I said, you're 30 years old, are you planning on having a family? He said yeah, I hope so – you plan on, you know, being able to travel? Do you plan on hospital insurance and stuff like that? Yeah. Well I said, what are you doing to be able to provide for your children? Do you plan on having your kids go to college? You do need to think about that. You need to think about the fact that I could get, you know, I could hire a nurse to go in and take care of my grandfather when he was dying. If one of my sisters got into trouble right now, I could help them. I can sit down and write a check if somebody is in dire dire need, and um, I think that's huge and I want to bring up, um, Claudia's mom right now – Danny can you come up here for a second, I'm going to go ahead and... speak. Can you pull this out? Can you pull a chair out too?

Um, some of you know about – that we had a huge vacation in Hawaii, because your children will never be the same when they get around these other people, and actually our next event, we're going to be smarter and learn from this event. What we're going to have is like a day care room, because I want your children playing with the children from Japan, and I want your children talking to my niece and nephew.

When we were in Hawaii, Jordi and Kurtie, didn't we go swim with the dolphins? Yeah. Okay, we're going to come back to you. What does he call you, Nanna or Granny? So, you were telling me yesterday. I want some close-ups of this pretty woman, okay?

Yesterday Steve and Claudia had a barbecue, the house was unbelievable, it was beautiful, I called one of my friends and said hey let me see how smart you are, can you figure this out? It was about a stubby and a tinnie and – the snag. And they thought it was hilarious too, said I can't understand anything they're saying, but you were talking to my mom.

**FEMALE:** Yes I did – I think every parent would be proud of their children, my daughter Claudia and my son in law Steve, invite them up since they met you. From the day they started with you, Steve has listened to you and from that day on, they proceed up and up and up and never gone backwards.

**CHRIS:** What did you see happening?

**FEMALE:** A lot of changes in their lives, in their um, attitude, oh yes, attitude, um, everything. And also, they used to live in the little unit, from the unit they went into the house, now they live in a big house, they're comfortable and they're very happy, which is what it's all about. You see your children happy and they grow, and it's the biggest riches in the world. Also my grandson he's going to be a beautiful young man.

[applause]

**CHRIS:** Now did you – when they first told you what they needed to do, were you scared?

**FEMALE:** Not really.

**CHRIS:** Because my parents were petrified, they were so afraid my dreams, the rug was going to be pulled out from me, I was going to be disappointed. I was going to be taken for my money.

**FEMALE:** I was not afraid of that because I had been in the same business years before that, but I only just managed, I didn't make so much money that I could live comfortably and all that, but since they started with Chris Carley, everything is going up and up and up – Steve is very intelligent and takes notice of you and does everything. Everything. It's true.

**CHRIS:** Have we rehearsed this at all? [laughter]

**FEMALE:** No, I am a very straight forward, honest person, I am very proud of my children, my family.

**CHRIS:** When are you going to get started?

**FEMALE:** Working? Well, I don't think I can be in too many places at a time, I'm helping my brother, helping Claudia with Bradley, they need support and I'm there.

**CHRIS:** I've been watching you and I'm going to take away some of your excuses, because we talked about time management... are you helping your brother because he's sick?

**FEMALE:** Yes, because he's sick, very sick.

**CHRIS:** Can you imagine where if you were also helping him but in addition to just doing a tiny bit extra that you could bring in the finest doctors, you could fly him to the finest research clinics?

**FEMALE:** Yes, for instance, you ca help people who will accept your help but if they don't want to accept your help, you can do nothing.

**CHRIS:** You've got to go on, but you could bring in a care taker where you could spend quality time and they could do all the work you don't want to do.

**FEMALE:** Yes, I organized before he came to the hospital, but um, they don't want that so I can't do anymore.

**CHRIS:** They've got you doing everything. What I'm trying to do here is, so many of us – what happened to my grandfather was, as they start to get sick, they will usually die of malnutrition just because they can't keep the food down or whatever, and I hired you know, somebody to go in there and feed him the nutrition that he needed, and my grandmother wouldn't let him in and there was nothing I could do. But I could have a big enough income to where, I get to take my family to Australia, I get to take the ones that are willing to live and willing to go on, I get to do that. Family is the hardest, family and friends. That's why you want to get your family and friends. My family and friends right now, if they want to get involved with my business, I give them to somebody else. We're out and having dinner, I have a question – no, I'm not going to talk about that, I have a life, you want to talk about that, this is the package, and we don't talk about it and they keep bringing it up, I say okay, why don't we talk about your job? I don't want to talk about my job, I've been there all day long. But a lot of motivation was, one, I didn't want to be – when you do get older, I didn't want to ever worry that I would be put away in a home, I wanted to be able to have a future that I could pass no – you create a strong, strong business, you get to pass that on to your kids, you can also skip your kids if they're not helping and doing things and listening, and give it to somebody else... but you've got to keep that in mind and this is the why, and also the why was, you know, to take care of my grandfather, to have enough money if I could, or let's say Jordi or Kurtie something happens to them. I've got a friend where they're at the mercy of charity because they can't afford to have these tests done because the insurance won't cover what happened to the child. Got something wrong – it's hard, something wrong with its brain, I hear it all the time, so you want to have a financial, security block, that doesn't count on anyone but yourself and then to secure your family, and I think that's why you feel good too, is that you don't have to worry about these two.

**Female:** Absolutely, that's the biggest point, you don't have to worry how they're going to pay their bills and all that, that's all covered. That's the biggest thrill that you can see your children prosper.

**Chris:** How do you feel when they say, hey mom, guess where I'm at, I'm in Hawaii, I'm in Malibu.

**Female:** My heart is tingling, I couldn't be happier for them.

**Chris:** Okay, Jordi and Curdi, do you remember going to Hawaii? Did you like that? Do you remember playing with all the other kids, and my niece? Did you kiss a dolphin? Did you get to swim and touch and hold them? Remember the turtles? Can you get on these two kids' faces? Remember when you didn't want to kiss the dolphin because it had bad breath? But you got to pet him, huh. Did you get to feed the turtles? What else did we do? We got to go out to dinner at Beni Hannah and we watched that guy flip shrimp all over your dad. Did you get to meet all the other kids too? What are you doing right now, emailing Sulley?

Yeah, you're talking to her on the computer. Weren't you in the pool and I was pulling you around, you had Kurtie's feet, Kurtie had someone else's feet, some of these kids in the pool didn't even speak English, and they were yapping. Guess who's going to take over your business? Our kids. And you can give them the stuff now. What was your favorite part of the whole thing? When you're in the pool, yeah. What about, um, when you went out to dinner every night. Some of the big producers in our field, their kids, you know, are there. Every single holiday we get to get together and somebody else pays for it – they get to experience, grow, see there's a bigger world, there's more than just us. These kids were whispering, then Kurtie and Jordi got in a fight over Sullivan, and I just want you guys to understand that life is just so huge, and you need to take experience with that, you need to see we're everywhere and we can effect and it's going to start with our children. Get your children to understand the value – don't give them the money, show them how to earn it. Everybody knows the saying I hope, I hope. Do not – give them a fish, eat for a day, teach them how to fish, he eats for the rest of his life. You've got to understand that you can do that and you can teach that to your children, and like your employees that you're going to have and the people in your life you're going to have, you are going to hurt them. Do you think every single time Claudia fell down, that Danny tried to catch her? Do you think every single time she had a question, she would do everything for her? When you're bringing somebody into the field of business and they're babies, you do not enable them, you do not have a life unless you teach these people to be strong. The worst thing you can do is tell that person the answer. I will have people come up to me and they'll say, what do I do here? I say, what do you think you would do? They've always got the right answer. So what does that mean, they want attention, they want to be stroked, what does that mean? They're human. I want attention, I want to feel good and I get it here.

**Female:** We're all humans, we want recognition and we also want the knowledge from people that we are doing the right thing, so that's—

**Chris:** you want to check in, tape yourself, listen, have other people listen, learn, you also want to be careful about what you're emulating, you want to emulate success.

[presentation continues]

You know, I used to just bang my head harder on it – that fly – let me find another open doorway. So sometimes it doesn't work out the way I want. Sometimes it takes longer what I want, but it just always seems to be because that was the reason why it should be. I don't understand that but I'm going to trust in the universe, I'm going to trust in the fact that I think what goes around comes around and um, if it doesn't happen, if something doesn't happen, there's a reason for it and I'm going to figure it out because I don't want to go through it again. Thank you so much.

## APPENDIX

# 2

# Interview of Chris Carley by the Network Marketing Magazine, Small Business Big Goals

**CHRIS:** Dominique?

**DOMINIQUE:** Yes, ma'am. Are you there?

**CHRIS:** Oh, good.

**DOMINIQUE:** Sorry about that. Oki doki. So, let's go ahead and get this ball rolling.

**CHRIS:** Okay, great.

**DOMINIQUE:** So, what are some of your most recent goals?

**CHRIS:** Oh, boy. I have a more enriched life. I've been taking care of my mom and dad. My dad just recently died. I just bought this place in Hawaii so I just want to appreciate all of the things that I've been getting, by also looking for purpose and passion, good friendships, good relationships and find something to do with all this money.

*Chris talking about spirituality*

**DOMINIQUE:** Do you feel that it is easy for someone to lose track of their spirituality while building their business?

**Chris:** I didn't find it that way because you know, I got a call yesterday, group of people that have been struggling in the same company I am in, and you know, they're in their 50s and 60s now, and they asked me about the same thing, "Well, you don't have to read everyday now, do you? or listen to motivational tapes or study and learn because you got it all" and I said. "No. You can never let up on that, you have to be because you're going to run across somebody and you're going to need the wisdom to be able to help them, and you're going to run across somebody that's angry and you need that guidance to get them and yourself back to a good place."

It's constant. It's everywhere and so anyways, usually people don't seem to turn to their spirituality unless something horrible is happening in their life. And then they're on their knees, but the trick is to keep on your knees during the whole time either thanksgiving and appreciation or "show me the way" because I don't know how to help this person and this person is struggling, and everything I've done is not working with them, and I need a new skill, I need to be better.

**CHRIS:** My favorite motivational speaker is named Jim Rohn. He is famous for saying the "For things to change, you have to change. For things to get better, I have to get better." You know, I have to be smarter and better and that's how I feel, like each level you go to, there's actually bigger events than things happening to you, like world hunger, when you're aware, clean water for people, and it's a lot.

**DOMINIQUE:** Absolutely.

**DOMINIQUE:** What are some things that you have put in place now so that you can make sure that you never forget to be spiritual or to always climb on your rock.

**CHRIS:** Some days, you feel like you don't need to be spiritual, you get whacked on the head. You need that. You need to connect and you need to understand that there's a universal intelligence, that this isn't random, otherwise, I don't know how you make it through the day. I just think that you have to constantly, like drinking water, you know, and eating. You have to feed your brain, feed your soul.

*Chris's advice on business*

**DOMINIQUE:** What would be three key points of advice that you would give a rising star in business, both personal and in business?

**CHRIS:** Free samples. You have to have products that you absolutely believe in, that have changed people's lives dramatically, emotional and physically. And if you have a product, you have to have a product, you have to be behind the product that no matter what, you would still be using even if the company has gone under.

Once you have that, then it's easy. I mean that person what they can give somebody, it's just karmic spirituality. If I can help somebody who's got a broken home or abusive husband or whatever problems of life, I am happy to. I deal with this daily. I mean, I have 120,000 people down line. I've got a lot of people coming at me. I'm supposed to be able to give them answers. That's when I turn to God. I have all this success, it's insignificant compared to Him.

**DOMINIQUE:** Definitely.

**DOMINIQUE:** So, why would you say that having God as first is the most important aspect in self-development and business ?

**CHRIS:** Because if you don't have that connectedness to the universe, to the creations, to why we're here and what are our purposes and where we are all going afterwards, you're a lost soul. You're just lost. You're sick and you're depressed and you have relationships that don't work out, and when you're connected to the spirit, to God, to the source, then you know when somebody's yelling at you for no reason. You don't have to get upset.

I've been reading the books and going to classes. I go to theology and church and I just study. When I do feel anger coming, I know I have to take a step back. When I was younger I was angry at my mother for forcing me to go to church and Bible camp. She used to say, "You're going to appreciate this one day." I have to thank her for it, because I have years and years of doctrine instilled in me that there is a higher purpose. There is a path of when you're connected to God.

**DOMINIQUE:** Would you say that there's a correlation between your spiritual growth and your growth within your business?

**CHRIS:** Well, you know back when I was really hitting it out of the ball park and now, I look back on it,

I'm just, "You haven't done that. It was God. It wasn't you." Back then, I thought I was doing the focusing on the law of attraction, universal intelligence, changing my thoughts and that attracted me all this money, but it just was never smooth.

It was a fight and it was rocky and it was people slinging rocks at you, and if only I would have turned to the Word and remembered my Bible training that this isn't about me, this is about them. So, I wish I would have. Each time I felt so alone and so exhausted, and I was helping thousands and thousands of people travelling around the world, why wasn't anybody helping me?

So, now, I can look back at it. I can say, you know, it would have been a much more fun ride and I would have enjoyed it a lot more if I would have had Him first here in my life. It's almost like a protective energy around you that lifts you. It's not only yourself but other people, it lifts them up.

**DOMINIQUE:** Absolutely.

*Chris on mastering marketing*

**DOMINIQUE:** So, shifting gears a little bit, talk more about mastering marketing, why is it important to know the basics in marketing when you're dealing with business?

**Chris:** Because I think I've gone to network marketing meetings and I've checked out five or six major competitors and what they were doing, and I found out that the people that came in when the company opens were the only ones making the big checks.

These big checks were really built by the company;

they were on stage showing these big, big checks telling us to talk to ten people a day. Well, the company that I was in was 15 years old, so I did the math real quick and talking to ten people a day would never allow me to reach what they did, ever. How can I possibly do that? And I knew I had to talk to 10,000 people a day to be able to catch up to them.

So I had to go back to the library and I learned, okay, I need to have free samples in this. These companies are teaching people to buy a $4,000 order. You know? Become this level. And even your first attempt at retailing, I had six people that I called on weight-loss ads and feel better, and get paid to lose weight, and they all said the same thing to me which was, "Okay, we need $200 to be able to use," and I was broke. It was absolutely insane. So, the seventh person I called, her name was Linda Williams, and I said, "I'm calling about your free sample." Finally, this woman said, "Yeah, come on over and I'll give you some free samples."

And because the product works, it took like 20 minutes where you start to feel better. It had 21 herbs and one of them was an antidepressant, in there was a little bit of stimulant. I felt great, and people don't teach that from the stage. They teach you to go out gals and guys, make as much money as you can, and then that's why everybody's got a bad conversation about network marketing. Everyone believes that it's just a pyramid scheme.

There are so many companies I'm sure they aren't, but they are all still teaching the same faulty thing. Talk to ten people a day. I stood up at one and said, "I want to know how you fill the room." You know, when you had people come to a meeting and they were talking about and I filled the room and "What did your ad say? Where did you place it?" you know? "How did you handle the call when it came in?" and they wouldn't answer me.

I mean, I was standing up, and I couldn't take it anymore. I was sleeping five girls to a hotel room, I was in the bath tub, all my last money to come to a California training with 40,000 people there and nobody to train us on how to do this business. So I learned the basic things on my own; that you need free samples, you need a money-back guarantee, you need to give value, you need to help that person make money, and get every sale but then also make money in their first four days.

**DOMINIQUE:** Right.

**CHRIS:** Because if you don't add them the whole machine breaks down, and it's pretty simple basic marketing, and you talk about this, and what I've written, if you look at any commercial or any that comes in your mail or let's just say the Pizza Hut comes up, you know? They don't advertise $19 for pizza, they advertise the lowest $9 thing and then you call in, then the upsell it's like, okay, this is how much it is for Coke.

**DOMINIQUE:** Right.

**CHRIS:** And they also do something that's very smart. They deliver the pizza, then they have a flyer in there to buy another pizza. You know? That's called follow-up, and then I'm sure I'm on a mailing list. That's very, very smart and so I incorporated all these. They are telling us to talk to ten people a day and do ten pitches a day, and each one took an hour, that's a 10-hour work day.

**DOMINIQUE:** Yeah.

**CHRIS:** So, I was just like, forget this. I'm going to have to take care of myself. Then as I gained success I found myself, repeating myself. So then I said, okay, I need to write, because this needs to get out there.

**DOMINIQUE:** That's awesome.

**CHRIS:** I mean even Microsoft, Dell, AT&T, they all advertise a low price to get you in the door and then get you on upgrades and referrals and returning. Copy the big boys is what I'd say.

**DOMINIQUE:** Oh yeah.

*Chris's take on getting into business*

**DOMINIQUE:** So, how would you describe business to someone who has never looked into starting their own business?

**CHRIS:** Well, I had never looked into starting my own business. I would tell them to think about what your life is now because as a factory worker, you had to have permission to go to the bathroom. You know, I worked midnight to seven. I was working in a huge airplane hangar with primarily men, and it was a bad environment. If you check-in one minute late, after that bell, you got written up. Three of them and you're fired.

I would say now, think about working at home, and it's a no-brainer, but I would caution people to not quit their job until they were losing money by going to work. I really do believe that because then you'll need that momentum.

I was telling my group the other day, I said, "Listen, I know you guys. This is hard work but this is worth it.

You just work hard for a few years and then you reinvest. A lot of people will get up there and get going. They'll be making money and when they start to succeed they just blow the money. Not reinvesting back into their advertising, and not reinvesting back into their people, and I call them up and say, "Look, you told me you'd listen to me. I got you to $30,000 a month. Now, I'm telling you, we only have this ride and we don't know how long it's going to last. We need to go for it." They wouldn't listen to me and have lost millions.

**DOMINIQUE:** Wow.

**DOMINIQUE:** I know you said, "Look at how the big boys do it," how would you advise someone to make a marketing strategy that will work best for them and their work flow?

**CHRIS:** Well, it's always the same. I mean, if you see what Pizza Hut's doing and you know that McDonald's doing the same thing, that Porsche same thing, that AT&T, Microsoft, Dell. I mean, you'll think of buying one thing and then all of a sudden, you've got 4-5, you know?

Even Internet connections, all of a sudden, you now got DirecTV, your phone, and you got this and somehow, my bill's huge every single month. They just have to start with a product that... you got to have a product that gets results. You don't have to have a product, it even works for a realtor. You must do your follow-up. I had a big 3 Million place in Malibu around the ocean, if I ever needed some place in the winter. I wanted to go to enjoy Trump International and move to Palm Beach so I called a realtor and said I'm just looking for a million dollar house. I want it on the water, and she said, "Well, we don't have one for that." And I said, "Okay, thank you.

Goodbye."

She lost a $2 million commission. The next person did the same thing and they said there's no way you can get a house on the ocean for that. So, I hung up and the third lady said, "Okay, yeah, sure. Come on out." And she showed me the shittiest worst house I've ever seen in my life. And then she showed me a 2 million dollar house that was brand new and beautiful on the ocean, perfect spot, so I went ahead and threw another million.

You just have to be smarter than the average sales person. These are basic marketing errors. You say, "No problem." to anybody that calls you and you feel that you've got the skills to teach them and do it, and you still you have the product, like these realtors. They didn't have the skills, they might have the product because these were the same houses that they were talking about, Palm Beach is a very small area. So, it's like, "Wow, you just lost that commission because you were too arrogant, or you thought maybe I wasn't serious... " it's just you can't pre-judge people willing to spend a million, you know? You just show them that. Do exactly what she did and educate.

**DOMINIQUE:** So, let's switch gears a little bit. Earlier on, you talked about the law of attraction and attracting the money, what is the significance of a positive mindset?

**CHRIS:** Well, have you ever seen the video, "What the Bleep?"

**DOMINIQUE:** No.

**CHRIS:** Okay. You should write that down and it's incredible. This has been in all of the scientific magazines.

This happened years and years ago, but they took two drops of water and put them under two different microscopes. To one drop, they screamed ugly things. Yelling things to the drop of water 'you're a loser and you're too old to start a new career... ' whatever it was, whatever negative things that could be said. On the other drop they said nothing but kind and encouraging and loving, beautiful things to this drop of water. Well then they looked at them, the one that had heard the ugly stuff was this yellow, puffy, it was just gross, and the one that had heard the positive, this thing was a beautiful blue, white, shining crystal.

**DOMINIQUE:** Wow.

**CHRIS:** And that really, really got me because when I was in the 5th Grade, I had this teacher that influenced my life. He did a similar experiment. He brought in two plants and we had to do the same thing. He said, "Okay, now every time you go by the one on the right, someone has to say, 'You can't do that and you're not going to grow.' And then this one over here, I want you to say loving kind words. Say, 'You know how beautiful you are and how strong you're going to get and how big you're going to get.'" In the end of that experiment, the sad plant died, and the other one flourished. It was something that really hit me.

**Dominique:** Wow.

**Chris:** An then I've read studies where scientists can hook up a rock that was in the Afghanistan war or any war where there is fighting going on, and they can pick up another rock that's in an environment of peace and loving and kindness, and the rocks show a difference in vibrations. Even though a rock has a really, really low vibration.

As humans we all have vibrations, each of us puts

out vibes. We hear because of the vibration in our ear drums, it's pure vibration. So as you vibrate at a different level, you drop the old vibration, it just falls off of you. You don't attract it anymore. The key though is to catch that vibration before it goes down. If I don't read for 4-5 days, I get up and I'm not feeling well. I'm not in a good mood and I'm just focusing on all the things that I've seen in my life that were horrendous, and I'm like, "Wait a minute!" So I go workout. I also go in and I listen to that still small voice within. I meditate and I read, or I listen or I watch something that is inspirational.

**DOMINIQUE:** That's awesome.

*Chris's take on positive mindset*

**DOMINIQUE:** So, with that same idea of positive mindset and really like working on staying positive at all times, how would you describe your natural personality versus the person you have worked to be at this point?

**Chris:** Well, the other personality was whining. There was a cloud over my head, what's the purpose in life. Back then I always thought of money. I just thought money would change everything. If I just had that money things would be different. Now I have that money and some days I still feel sad, because of focusing on all of the people. I didn't help all the people that I tried to take with me, who fought me, and they were left behind.

They wouldn't read the books of mine, they wouldn't go to the events like Wayne Dyer or Tony Robbins, or someone like that. They didn't grow and now they're still struggling. So the difference is that now, I can change quicker. If I find that there are things not going right in my life.

So, I stop and say, "Okay, what is that? What am I doing?" and pray about it and ask guidance about it and every time negative thoughts come into my mind, I have to remember, "Okay, I'm not alone. I'm not alone. And I'm okay." I just sit and write out everything I'm thankful for. That seems to keep me on the right track.

**DOMINIQUE:** So, what works?

**CHRIS:** It makes me smoother, lighter, and happier and clearer. You also have to watch who you're listening to and not let people go on and on about their problems. Do not watch movies that are negative. I even have trouble watching the news. I don't know how anybody could live in a peace, calm state if you're watching the news and hearing what people do to each other. So in my mind I have my own channel, a channel about wonderful people that made big differences in my life. I see bad things going on in the world and this person I know donated his wealth to this African village. You know that touches you. I realized I had to go visit those places too. See how my money can help these people get out of prosecution and get clean water.

**DOMINIQUE:** That's awesome.

*Chris's best advice for you*

**DOMINIQUE:** What will be some of the best advice that you can give someone to stay focused on the positive because I know you're saying that people get distracted by everything that's happening.

**CHRIS:** You know, it's so simple. It's so simple, but I can't get people to do it and you have to read daily. I try to do it three times a day, once when you wake up to get your mind going. It's not like it takes a lot, you could reading in the bathroom, you know?

You're there anyway, take the time to read it. I got into an argument with this guy that I was running promotions for. I have spent over $50,000 in promotions and he's great. He brings people in. He's good with the people. He does everything he's supposed to do, but he doesn't ever hit it big.

I was like, "Hey, did you read that book I recommended? and he's like, "No, I can't, my girlfriend's going to get mad at me if she catches me reading and goofing off." I said, "You're not goofing off. Just go into the bathroom, do 8 minutes and read this chapter I told you to read." Another time I was running a $10,000 promotion I put out to my group and said, "Hey, I want you guys to skip ahead and go to this chapter and read it, and then get back to me." And for 5 days, nobody got back to me and so, I said, "You guys all just lost $10,000." You don't have to worry about where it's going to come from, you just got to picture the outcome, and if you're not doing that, that means you're not reading the books I'm telling you to read.

**DOMINIQUE:** So, reading is probably the number one thing that is the difference between success and failure?

**(THERE IS NO ANSWER HERE.)**

**CHRIS:** So, I do have many, many people tell me, "I'm an awful reader. I don't like to read. I hate reading." Well then, "listen to this book or that book on tape...

**Dominique:** Right.

**CHRIS:** This is for you, you know."

I can take away everybody's excuses. I have had one distributor who had to leave her husband with… she had 3 kids, she was living out of her car, did not have a phone number, and the person that sponsors her wanted me to help her, so I said, "Okay, park your car by a phone booth and go within a radius of where you can see your car. Go give out these flyers" and it's very important that you're advertising free samples, lose weight, feel great, money-back guarantee. So she put down the phone number of the payphone she was calling from and within 4 days had made enough money to go in and get a new apartment.

**DOMINIQUE:** Wow. That's amazing.

**CHRIS:** It is and it's cool and it's like I had to remember those stories. I got to remember it. I have a blind guy that I made a little 14-page book. He was legally blind but could only see a tiny bit, but he has a computer, and just reads one word at a time. One word taking up the entire computer screen. He has already written a couple of books and he did well with me. He's a great inspiration to all of us.

That's when I was struggling. I couldn't find a way to be successful, my mind was saying, "Gosh, I'm losing weight, I'm feeling great," but I didn't know what I was doing wrong and that's when I changed my approach. The other thing that happens when you're constantly absorbing these ideas and thoughts is that you create new pathways. You get inspiration and these directions pop up, that didn't exist before. "Oh, go get that back. Oh, call that person. Oh, no, don't stop at that restaurant." And it's just cool and strange, and it just seems like everybody around me was like, "What do you do, poop Diamonds out of you butt? How are you doing this?"

While you guys were watching TV, I'm at the library. I'm at the gym and I would see 8 or 9 of the cross lines that were from the competition. They'd be working out and wave me over, and I have my headphones on. And finally, about after a couple of months, somebody just grabbed my headphones and listened to what I was listening to. It was their CD, it was actually him. Because he was beating me at that time, I was "Of course, I'm studying you!"

**DOMINIQUE:** Absolutely.

**CHRIS:** And I said, "What are you guys listening to, I bet you're listening to a bunch of crap." And yeah, sure enough, they were. They were listening to nonsense. Music... no, I'm not saying music is nonsense but...

**DOMINIQUE:** They weren't listening to the thing that's going to help them so...

**CHRIS:** Right. Right.

*Chris's take on beating back the excuses*

**DOMINIQUE:** Okay. So, one of the excuses that people may come up with is that they have this family life that they need to uphold. How would you advise someone on having a family life and doing business?

**CHRIS:** Well, you can only do this again with a great, great product. At the time I had lost 42 pounds in 8 weeks. I was depressed. I had been fired from Boeing for complaining about the work environment, and it's just kind of hard to get off the couch. I got that little flyer and it was amazing so, anyway, I lost 42 pounds. My husband at the time, who's an ex now, was always trying to sabotage me. Unfortunately, you're going to have that in your family sometimes.

People are afraid. My father was afraid. My mother was, “Oh, she’s going to get scammed. Oh, she’s going to bring all these people, and then they all got a little company that’s going to fail and it’s a pyr–” it was a constant battle. So, I kind of just smiled at them and shut them up and said, “Yeah, yeah, yeah, but I lost 42 pounds. I feel great. I’m not depressed, and I’m out doing stuff, so what can this hurt anybody?” and then I got my mom on it, my dad on it, and my sister and they’d lost weight and they felt great. See, you got to involve your family. You have to make them part of this. You have to show them the big picture.

People think that there’s all this big thing to sales. Everybody is in sales. They are in sales trying to get their kids to do what they’re supposed to do, “If you do this, I’ll do this. If you do this, you’ll get this.” You know, husband-wife relationships? Those things you’re selling yourself, “Look, I know what I’m doing. This I what I want to do.” and if you’d read the books that I’ve read, then we would be on the same level, we wouldn’t be fighting and we’ll be okay.

So, know when somebody does give you the opposition that they’re just scared. I mean, I grew up in a family where my grandfather was at Boeing, my father was a Boeing employee. There’s a hundred years of my family at Boeing, at a factory as a factory worker. The bad part is that it was always financially stressful growing up. You got laid off a couple of times but always, money was tight. I remember one day going out in a field falling over a rock. I saw this gold in some rocks so I got my dad’s little wheelbarrow. I could barely wheel it and I loaded it up with all these gold rocks I thought I had found. I brought it to the front porch and I said, “Dad! Come out here. I've got a way for you to quit Boeing and for us to not to be afraid of bill paying." He came out and he tried not to laugh.

**CHRIS:** So from that age on, I remember him telling me, "Dad, who's the richest man that you know of?" he says, "Why? I guess it would be Donald Trump." And I would remember walking to school and thinking about Donald Trump and maybe what if I could meet him and he would give me some tips on business, and wouldn't it be great to have that and my family not have to work and we could be together.

In my 30's, I was the first ever single woman to join the "Mar-a-Lago Club" and Trump International. Donald introduced me to golf. He set me up with golf lessons. He introduced me to people, everybody accepted me, and I was beaming. It was great. So, those are all these visualization pictures of how powerful the subconscious is.

When I was running promotions I only put money into people who I was suggesting to that if you read this book, I'll buy you this ad. I already knew that they were trained. I already knew they knew how to… they loved their product. I also knew they understood the basics of marketing. So, I would buy them the ad, because they're going to make me millions and so I was like, "Okay, but I would never do it on values. If you did $20,000, this is what the company's deal was, you'll get a picture with the owner and you'll get to have dinner with all the top people." That's not going to help you next month.

**DOMINIQUE:** That's true.

**CHRIS:** It's insane. Give them an ad, give them

flyers, give them internet or something. It's so simple. You put your money back into these people, but if they had learned in these years to put money back in, it would be a different story. I also read with my group. For instance I would send a message out, "Did you read chapter 14 where Joel senses that God's grace is going to shine on him and we're his children and he wants our life to be on earth as it is in heaven," and so, we get in this big discussion group and we all watch the DVD. If I'm listening to someone, whether it's Wayne Dyer or whoever it is, then everybody else is, "Okay, I'm listening to it too."

We would get this big energy thing going and we're all encouraging each other and, "Hey, I just signed up another person. Hey, I just got them to pay my ads for doing this." And that's really important. In my own upline, both the woman and the one above, they never called me when I hit key levels. There's no encouragement, no 'atta-girl.' There is nothing wrong with giving somebody some accolades. In fact, this makes them grow like that plant when you tell them beautiful things about themselves.

**DOMINIQUE:** Absolutely. Absolutely. I agree with you 1,000%.

*Chris on time management*

**DOMINIQUE:** So there are people reading the book and they have all these things going on and now, time is starting to become an issue because they're putting all of their time in all these different things, so they can market themselves effectively, how would you advise someone to better manage their time?

**Chris:** This is so simple and so sad. The reason

most businesses fail is fear of rejection and so you have to take away all the rejections. So when we were selling a product, our message was, "If you're serious about wanting to lose weight or feel better or make money from your phone, are you serious?" and if they didn't say yes, we'd say, "Okay, we care about you and we'll put you on the free newsletter. Call me when you are serious."

And that sets the tone. We're like, "Okay, now, I'm not going to be on the phone with you. I'm not going to be able to do this. You have to do this, this and this training, and then you can have a call where I can talk to you." so, what was happening was they're talking about getting 10 No's a day, and so I was like, "There's got to be a way to not have those No's, not to have that rejection."

So then, we had a system where we gave them our 14-page booklet about "Don't you want to find money in your mailbox everyday? Don't you want to have a job that if you get sick or divorce or death in the family, where your check still comes in and maybe even grow to double?" Pitching them this idea of residual income, royalties really and so, when the person got them reading that book, if they weren't in our vibration, if they weren't having the same goals and dreams that we have in our hearts, they wouldn't call us, right? They just toss it.

I actually had a guy come in off of a booklet he found in the garbage in a gas station. By the end of one year he was making 7 or 8,000 dollars a month.

So, the time management is we cut away all that wasted time. In the industry they tell you, you have to call 20 people back. I was like, "No, you're not calling anybody back, they have to call you." Now, we know they're a little bit interested. Okay now we're going to send the package, it has another book in it, it has a video, and an audio. It's all going to be about "working-at-home". All the positive reasons and about what's happening. Explaining it to them about what's happening to somebody that works with a company that could go under, all those things.

So, then they got to go through all the material; book, the video, and the audio. If they don't now want to come into your business, they don't call you, you don't get rejected. But if they do say, "This is it, this is it. What do I do next?" Well then, we send them another package that tells them about the company and the product, and then guess what? They call us and they say, "I want to come in at this level."

That's how we did it. II'm talking my income didn't just double or triple, it went crazy. After we all started using the marketing tools I created, it jumped to over $100,000 a month.

**DOMINIQUE:** Wow.

**CHRIS:** A month.

**DOMINIQUE:** That's amazing. That is amazing.

**CHRIS:** Yeah. No college, no business experience, no successes in my life

**DOMINIQUE:** Wow. That is amazing.

**CHRIS:** And that's because we got rid of all the people that weren't in our vibration, all the people that didn't have this same thinking process like us. It wouldn't resonate with all those types of people. Everybody likes to mail out the business opportunity mailers, I do not like to do that. I want motivational people that have read the books I've read. Then, it's an easy swim. It's just doing laps, I mean. You know, and I didn't work more than3-4 hours a day. When the internet came in, like another explosion, it just kept going.

**DOMINIQUE:** So, on average, how long do you say that you would work on a project or work on one aspect of business? So, a work day instead of being from 9 to 5, how long would it be?

**Chris:** I don't like to talk to anybody until after 10 because I wake up slowly, about 7. I have to go for a walk and I have to do my reading and sitting, just enjoy the morning. I start work around 10 to 3. I find that I'm teaching people that you don't have to have your family where you're gone 12 hours a day or you're on the phone 12 hours a day, or you're in a boiler room type of atmosphere. That's what too many people are doing.

I remember when we didn't have cell phones. I lived in an apartment so I bought an extra long extension cord. I would take the phone down to the apartment's pool. Everybody's at work so I was at the pool all by myself. For years I've been talking to people and saying, "Yes, you can take charge of your time. You must believe in you."

I had this gal as a waitress and her name is Amber. She lost, I think, 30-some pounds and she had a 2 year-old boy and I would say, "Amber, this is crazy. Don't you want to stay home with your boy? You don't even see your husband. I was a waitress so I know what you're making in tips, I'm telling you, you can just work 3-4 hours from your home and make as much as you were at work, I swear and you'll be around your son and your husband."

Her husband didn't want her to do it and I said, "Look, I have 5 leads for you right now that all want to buy the product that you bought. It's only $30 and give them a free sample, same thing I did with you."

By the way, there should be no training. You shouldn't need training in this industry because you are trained by the way you were brought in. So, she got on the free samples, she got on the $30 product and she wanted more product and I said, "You have to register at the company so you can buy it for wholesale for yourself." And I made her independent immediately because I did not want a returning resale customer. It's going to waste my time and my energy.

I wanted an independent distributor. I want them to make their own money, if they said they were serious. That was an important thing. I find that I always needed them to say that, because I can remind them, "Look, you said you were serious. Amber, you told me you're serious about making this much extra money. Now, are you going to listen to me or what? I've got 5 leads for you, you can go home and get them done within an hour and you have made more than you would tonight at work." And I proved it.

**DOMINIQUE:** Wow.

*Chris's take on working smarter not harder*

**DOMINIQUE:** What would you say is the difference between working hard and working smarter?

**CHRIS:** Take one guy that I know who is working from 6AM till midnight and he's on boiler room type calls. They have these training calls. Monday, Wednesday,

Saturday and on Thanksgiving he called me and I said, "Happy Thanksgiving!" he goes, "Oh yeah, I forgot it's Thanksgiving. I'm working, I'm in the office." I was like, "What?! Why aren't you with your family?" you know, he was in the same state.

He'd phone in to do another meeting. I said, "Sheesh, you got way too many meetings, way too many conference calls. Get these people independent." They were dog-piling on leads from anybody that wants the opportunity or... it is just not the same as it is when you're getting leads from somebody that has read Joel Osteen's books or "Think and Grow Rich", or anything like that. You don't have to do that part. And if you set it up to where you don't need any training, because I brought you in is the way you're going to bring in the next person the same way.

I remember another time seeing one of my guys pitching a waitress and trying to do the whole marketing thing right there at the table. I walked over to him and said, "John, stop it!" I handed the girl a book and said, "Look, here's to losing weight, feeling better, and making more money. Read this book to follow directions." That's it.

What's happening is this girl is tuned out. First of all, her eyeballs are rolling back in her head. Second of all, I've known John for a year. He's brought in hundreds of people this way. These people can't duplicate what he's done. They're not able to talk like that. Some people don't like to talk, some people don't know how. So we did the talking for them. It may be my training videos, while I'm sleeping, and while my group is sleeping, that's the stuff that's working for them and doing all the work. Anything that they have to say, we have it here.

Everything we've covered it and if we didn't cover it, we'll put it in there.

Third, John's style made everybody uncomfortable, you know? Everywhere we go and no matter where we'd be at, he'd be talking to some vendor or some person. It was just crazy but a whole lot of people are like that. Early on I was noticing that some people in my group just didn't understand this strategy. I couldn't get them to listen to me no matter what, they had lost weight, they felt great, they were making 5 or 6,000 a month, but they wouldn't listen to me, and they were stuck. John was one of those people.

So I found someone underneath him and I started helping her. I started getting her to use the materials. This strategy took away all the rejections, took away all the talking, and put a 10-hour day down to 3-hours or 4-hours for her. She passed them all up and she never looked back. She was up there at $30,000 a month and John got a little bit bigger because of her, but not much. To this day, I can't do anything to help him.

**DOMINIQUE:** So, when did you realize that you could work smarter and how did you make the change between working hard?

**CHRIS:** Right away. My first event leaders were on stage showing their checks and nobody was telling us how, nobody was saying "This is how I did it. This is what I used to advertise." You know, they're telling you to go talk to friends and family and that is the hardest thing you could ever do in your life. Friends and family that know you and have seen all your failures – that is the worst thing you can do. In fact, the worst thing you can do is pitch your product to anybody. They should be asking you.

They should be, "Oh my gosh, you've lost 30 pounds. Oh my gosh, you look great. Oh, you're radiating. You're skin is incredible." What's going on with you? You shouldn't have to be bugging your friends and family. They should be coming to you. And then, you've taken control of it and you have to be precious with your time. Use the system, then tell them to call you when they are serious. Then you're not dragging and pulling people.

**DOMINIQUE:** Right.

**DOMINIQUE:** We're going to shift gears again. Okay. I know earlier, you were talking about you would tell people like, "Hey, here's the information. Call me when you're serious." right?

**CHRIS:** Right.

**DOMINIQUE:** And some people would call, some people wouldn't. Now, with people that would change their minds after taking more into consideration, what do you think or how can one shift their mindset so that they can better receive the information that you give them after that point?

**CHRIS:** Good question. I think that everybody has it inside of them, you know? They have God inside of them, the Creator that created all this and that person is in your life for some reason. You run into this person and if you're reading the books and you're meditating and praying and stuff, you'll know exactly what to say that will resonate in them and that would ignite that. And a lot of times with my people, it was like, "Okay. When you're serious, give me a call and I'll help you." and I would send them an update.

I would say, "Amber just did $5,000 a month and John

did $7,000, and this person did this and this person lost this much weight." You know back then we didn't have an email address and stuff like that, so I had to actually hand mail them.

**DOMINIQUE:** That is so awesome. It's so interesting to hear how you've overcome all these things and how you can reflect on them in the way that you do because it's like you're standing on a higher ground so you're able to talk about the things that you know, "This happened."

**CHRIS:** Yeah.

*Chris's take on maintaining your enthusiasm*

**DOMINIQUE:** So, let's see the next question I have here is how can a person work on their work stamina and by that, I mean not burning out before they get to the prize.

**CHRIS:** It's really the same thing. If you've got burned out, you're doing something wrong, and you're getting the wrong information, you're getting trained by the wrong people and I would just challenge everybody, before you listen to them, ask to see their check and ask when they came in to the company.

If you've got a company that hasn't had people with a significant amount of success within the first two or three years, there's something wrong with what's going on with the company. If that company always has the same people on the stage as leaders, year after year, you're listening to the wrong advice. You're listening to the wrong thing. And if you're burning out, you're doing something wrong. You have to make it fun, you have to make it light, you have to say, you know, there's no problem and you have to know your stories too.

You must know the story of the blind guy who read one word at a time and the woman living in her car. There's just hundreds and hundreds of stories like that everywhere. You want to identify them and with somebody that touches their soul and reaches to the core of their heart. Then they say, okay, that person did it. These people did it.

If I had a truck driver, I'd call up my friend who was making the big bucks, he was also a truck driver, and I'd call and I'd say, "Well, you know you're driving 10 hours day, how could you do this business?" "Are you kidding? I had a sign on the back of my truck." This would be inspiration for the new truck driver wanting to sign up.

I can remember after hearing that myself, I put a big sign on the back of my mom and dad's motor home. They were in a caravan with 5 other RVs it was wild, they were on the road and trucks would be honking at them. My mother was freaking out.

What happened is this. My dad and mom are thinking "What is it that you want?" My dad looks at the guy, first it looks like he's waving them to move over, then he wants them to pull over. My dad tells my mom "What the heck?" And she says, "He keeps pointing to the back end, the back end, and Dad's, "Oh, that's Chris's poster!" so then he made a sale with this truck driver.

He stopped at the next rest stop and he shows his weight loss pictures and he shows my checks to the truck driver and tells him to "Just call her. She'll help you." He's done that everywhere, all over the Washington state.

**DOMINIQUE:** Wow. That's so awesome.

**CHRIS:** But you know, you also got to create a sense of excitement and belonging in a family-type atmosphere where again, you care about each other and helping each other and you work in cross line because you know it's going to come back to you. You know, 10 fold. I think that was what the Bible says. So, you got to remember that for every act of random kindness, you might not get it back from that person but you will get it back and it will come back to you, joy and happiness and other right ideas will come to you, all of a sudden you meet the right person and it just all comes together for you.

**DOMINIQUE:** Absolutely. So, I think we're going to wrap it up with this last question. Let's see. I'm trying to think. Oh, here we go.

**DOMINIQUE:** When did you realize that quitting was not an option? And can you please share your one bold experience.

**CHRIS:** The quitting, what happens sadly is people go, they get excited, they're losing weight, they're feeling better, they're seeing all these checks, they were you know, full on for 30 to 90 days and then nothing is happening at times like that planting the seed, right? You don't see it growing down in the roots. You don't see it coming up but once it comes up, all of the sudden it will break through and it will shoot up.

But people, if they don't see any results and they quit, and they start seeing results, well then, they've lost their momentum and they have to start over. I don't believe in luck. I believe books brought me to the right opportunity and the right company, right person, I mean, I hung up on 5 or 6 other people that were selling the same thing. All of them lost earning money from my $20 Million in income. Even the person above me I passed her about 6 months after I started and never looked back. She never got to where I was.

That's also the proof of whether or not network marketing is a pyramid scheme. If you can make more than the person that brought you in, it's not a pyramid. At Boeing, you had a general manager who'd been there for whatever, 30 years. Then you would have a manager, followed by a supervisor. No matter who you were the only way I could get a pay raise was by time. I couldn't get it by anything else, you know, because the union and seniority. That was a true pyramid where you can't make more money than the person that's above you.

**DOMINIQUE:** Right. Alrighty. So, that was it for my questions. Was there anything else that you want to share?

**CHRIS:** Would you mind friending me on Facebook?

**DOMINIQUE:** Yeah.

**CHRIS:** Just put Chris Carley then put Kailua, K-A-I-L-U-A Kona Hawaii. And you'll see me. Friend me you'll be able to see my blog and my Twitter and all that stuff I've been putting out. We go ten times as fast now, as opposed to what I did when I had to mail out everything and I was broke. I didn't have the means to advertise, didn't have the internet. I didn't even have a fax machine. Twitter and social media didn't exist at all.

There's no reason why anybody can't do this if they

have the right product and if they have the right basic marketing training. Selling a low introductory product, free samples, money back guarantee, and then when they get results, they're going to need more product. That's when you register them and teach them how to do it on their own. And I have a lot of people that I registered throughout the years where they never did get excited about making money, but they're still buying and I still have $7-8,000 personal volume without doing anything for 10 years.

**DOMINIQUE:** Wow.

**CHRIS:** But they love the product and I planted that seed in them, and I help them, you know.

**DOMINIQUE:** Let's see. This might be you. You have like light brown, reddish hair?

**CHRIS:** Yeah.

**DOMINIQUE:** Alright. I just sent a friend request.

**CHRIS:** Oh, good.

**DOMINIQUE:** Oh, yeah it is. It's you. Cool. Cool.

**CHRIS:** Yeah. Okay, thank you so, so much.

**DOMINIQUE:** Yeah. No worries. I'll talk to you soon.

**CHRIS:** Okay.

**DOMINIQUE:** Yeah, definitely. B-bye.

**CHRIS:** B-bye.

CPSIA information can be obtained
at www.ICGtesting.com
Printed in the USA
LVOW12*1356120516
487956LV00002B/4/P

9 780966 624533